THE ARGUMENT FROM

A Reply to Legal Positivism

The Argument from Injustice

A Reply to Legal Positivism

Robert Alexy

translated by

Bonnie Litschewski Paulson and Stanley L. Paulson

OXFORD
UNIVERSITY PRESS

Great Clarendon Street, Oxford OX2 6DP

Oxford University Press is a department of the University of Oxford.
It furthers the University's objective of excellence in research, scholarship,
and education by publishing worldwide in

Oxford New York

Auckland   Cape Town   Dar es Salaam   Hong Kong   Karachi
Kuala Lumpur   Madrid   Melbourne   Mexico City   Nairobi
New Delhi   Shanghai   Taipei   Toronto
With offices in
Argentina   Austria   Brazil   Chile   Czech Republic   France   Greece
Guatemala   Hungary   Italy   Japan   South Korea   Poland   Portugal
Singapore   Switzerland   Thailand   Turkey   Ukraine   Vietnam

ISBN 978-0-19-958421-5

Printed in the United Kingdom by
Lightning Source UK Ltd., Milton Keynes

Translators' Preface

We are pleased to be able to make Robert Alexy's book, *Begriff und Geltung des Rechts*, available in English. During our work on the project, Professor Alexy was always more than open to questions and generous in discussing points of interpretation. We are confident that our joint effort has contributed substantially to both accuracy and idiom.

The title, *The Argument from Injustice. A Reply to Legal Positivism*, was chosen over a literal translation of the German title, *The Concept and the Validity of Law*, for several reasons. Not only does the latter lack the crisp ring of the German, it also seemed to us much too close to H. L. A. Hart's title, *The Concept of Law*. The new title is an accurate reflection of the focus of Alexy's book, a title that we hope speaks to a broad spectrum of readers interested in these issues.

One convention, our use of 'see' and 'at' in the footnotes, might be mentioned. When a footnote invites the reader to 'see' a particular place in a given work, that particular information is preceded by 'at'. Two variations are possible: 'see...at § 13 (pp. 67–9)' refers to all of § 13, which spans pp. 67–9, while 'see...§13 (at pp. 67–8)' refers to particular pages within § 13.

St Louis
September 2001

Bonnie Litschewski Paulson
and Stanley L. Paulson

Contents

Abbreviations

The abbreviations are divided into two alphabetical lists: first, abbreviations of titles of books and articles that are frequently cited, and second, abbreviations of all items in German law that are cited.

I. Books and Articles

Ak	*Akademie* edition. *Gesammelte Schriften* (Collected Writings) of Immanuel Kant, ed. by the Royal Prussian (later: 'German') Academy of Sciences (Berlin: de Gruyter, 1900–). Save for the *Critique of Pure Reason* (where the standard *A* and *B* pagination is used), we have adopted the pagination of the Academy edition, found in marginal entries of most translations. Works are cited with volume and page numbers, in the form *Ak* 1:10 (Academy edn., vol. 1, p. 10). The *Ak* citation follows a reference to a standard translation.
Alexy, *TCR*	Alexy, Robert, *A Theory of Constitutional Rights* (1st pub. 1985), trans. Julian Rivers (Oxford: Clarendon Press, 2002).
Alexy, *TLA*	Alexy, Robert, *A Theory of Legal Argumentation* (1st pub. 1978), trans.

Ruth Adler and Neil MacCormick
(Oxford: Clarendon Press, 1989).

Austin, *Lectures*   Austin, John, *Lectures on
                        Jurisprudence* (1st pub. 1863), 5th
                        edn., ed. Robert Campbell, 2 vols.
                        (London: John Murray, 1885, repr.
                        Glashütten im Taunus: Auvermann,
                        1972).

Austin, *Province*   Austin, John, *The Province of
                        Jurisprudence Determined* (1st pub.
                        1832), ed. with an introd. by H. L. A.
                        Hart (London: Weidenfeld and
                        Nicolson, 1954, repr. Indianapolis:
                        Hackett, 1998).

Dreier, *RMI*   Dreier, Ralf, *Recht—Moral—
                        Ideologie* (Law—Morality—Ideology)
                        (Frankfurt: Suhrkamp, 1981).

Hart, *CL*, [and *CL*] Hart, H. L. A., *The Concept of Law*
2nd edn.   (Oxford: Clarendon Press, 1961), and
                        2nd edn., with Postscript, ed. Penelope
                        A. Bulloch and Joseph Raz (Oxford:
                        Clarendon Press, 1994).

Hart, *Essays*   Hart, H. L. A., *Essays in Jurisprudence
                        and Philosophy* (Oxford: Clarendon
                        Press, 1983).

Hart, *PSLM*   Hart, H. L. A., 'Positivism and the
                        Separation of Law and Morals',
                        Harvard Law Review, 71 (1957–8),
                        593–629, repr. Hart, *Essays* (see
                        above), 49–87.

Hoerster, *LR*   Hoerster, Norbert, 'Die
                        rechtsphilosophische Lehre vom

Rechtsbegriff' (The Juridico-
Philosophical Theory of the Concept
of Law), *Juristische Schulung*, 27
(1987), 181–8.

Hoerster, *VR*   Hoerster, Norbert, 'Zur Verteidigung
des Rechtspositivismus' (On the
Defence of Legal Positivism), *Neue
Juristische Wochenschrift*, 39 (1986),
2480–2.

Hoerster, *VT*   Hoerster, Norbert, 'Zur Verteidigung
der rechtspositivistischen
Trennungsthese' (On the Defence of
the Legal Positivist's Separation
Thesis), in *RWR* (see below), 27–32.

Kelsen, *LT*   Kelsen, Hans, *Introduction to the
Problems of Legal Theory*, trans. of the
1st edn. of the *Reine Rechtslehre*
(1934) by Bonnie Litschewski Paulson
and Stanley L. Paulson (Oxford:
Clarendon Press, 1992).

Kelsen, *PTL*   Kelsen, Hans, *Pure Theory of Law*,
trans. of the 2nd edn. of the *Reine
Rechtslehre* (1960) by Max Knight
(Berkeley and Los Angeles: University
of California Press, 1967).

MEA   *Methodologie und Erkenntnistheorie
der juristischen Argumentation*
(Methodology and Epistemology of
Legal Argumentation), ed. Aulis
Aarnio, Ilkka Niiniluoto, and Jyrki
Uusitalo, *Rechtstheorie*, Beiheft
(suppl. vol.) 2 (Berlin: Duncker &
Humblot, 1981).

Radbruch, *GUR*   Radbruch, Gustav, 'Gesetzliches
Unrecht und übergesetzliches Recht'
(Statutory Non-Law and
Suprastatutory Law), in the
Süddeutsche Juristen-Zeitung, 1
(1946), 105–8, repr. in *RGA 3* (see
below), 83–93, 282–91 (editorial
notes).

Radbruch, *LP*   Radbruch, Gustav, *Legal Philosophy*
(1st pub. 1932), trans. Kurt Wilk in
*The Legal Philosophies of Lask,
Radbruch, and Dabin*, with an introd.
by Edwin W. Patterson (Cambridge,
Mass.: Harvard University Press,
1950), 43–224.

RGA 3   Radbruch, Gustav, *Gesamtausgabe*
(Collected Works), ed. Arthur
Kaufmann (Heidelberg: C. F. Müller,
1987–), vol. 3: *Rechtsphilosophie III*,
ed. Winfried Hassemer (1990).

RWR   *Rechtspositivismus und Wertbezug des
Rechts* (Legal Positivism and the
Reference of Law to Values), ed.
Ralf Dreier, *Archiv für Rechts- und
Sozialphilosophie*, Beiheft (suppl. vol.)
37 (Stuttgart: Franz Steiner, 1990).

II. German Law

BGB   *Bürgerliches Gesetzbuch* (German
Civil Code).

BGH   *Bundesgerichtshof* (Supreme Court of
the Federal Republic of Germany).

BGHSt	*Entscheidungen des BGH in Strafsachen* (Decisions of the Federal Supreme Court in Criminal Matters).
BGHZ	*Entscheidungen des BGH in Zivilsachen* (Decisions of the Federal Supreme Court in Civil Matters).
BVerfGE	*Entscheidungen des Bundesverfassungsgerichts* (Decisions of the Constitutional Court of the Federal Republic of Germany). Citations include vol. no., date, and page no(s).
GG	*Grundgesetz* (Basic Law or Constitution of the Federal Republic of Germany), trans. as *Basic Law* (Bonn: Federal Printing Office, 1964), repr., as amended to 1 Dec. 1993, in David P. Currie, *The Constitution of the Federal Republic of Germany* (Chicago and London: University of Chicago Press, 1994), 343–412. A later translation contains certain problematic changes (Berlin: German Bundestag—Administration, 2001).
OLG Bamberg	*Oberlandesgericht Bamberg* (Appeals Court, Bamberg).
RGBl	*Reichsgesetzblatt* (Statutes at Large of the German Reich).
RzW	*Rechtsprechung zum Wiedergutmachungsrecht* (Decisions on the Law of Indemnification). (This reporter was a supplement to the journal *Neue Juristische Wochenschrift*, vols. 1–32 (1949–81).)

Foreword

This book, written during a research semester, stems from a project of Ralf Dreier's and mine aimed at a short monograph on the general outlines of legal theory. Because the present work outgrew the scope of the single chapter envisaged in our joint project, I decided to publish it separately. For their encouragement, I wish to thank both Ernesto Garzón Valdés and Meinolf Wewel. And I extend special thanks to Ralf Dreier, whose long-standing influence can be seen in everything I have written here. The responsibility for mistakes is of course mine alone. I also wish to thank Heinke Dietmair for her unwavering patience and care in preparing the manuscript for the press, as well as Martin Borowski, Carsten Heidemann, and Marius Raabe for their help in reading the proofs.

Kiel   Robert Alexy
January 1992

Foreword to the English Edition

I had the chance, together with Bonnie Litschewski Paulson and Stanley L. Paulson, to compare their translation of my book, line for line, with the German text. The exercise splendidly confirmed the notion that translation is essentially interpretation. At many points, thanks to their formulations, I was better able to understand my book than when I drafted it. Our discussions occasionally led to questions that could not be resolved through mere interpretation, and I have altered the text accordingly. In each case, the reader is of course alerted to the alteration.

My thanks to the translators for all their effort cannot be overstated.

Kiel   Robert Alexy
September 2001

I

The Problem of Legal Positivism

1. The Basic Positions

The central problem in the debate surrounding the concept of law is the relationship of law and morality. Notwithstanding a discussion that reaches back more than two millennia,[1] there remain two basic, competing positions—the positivistic and the non-positivistic.

All positivistic theories defend the *separation thesis*, which says that the concept of law is to be defined such that no moral elements are included. The separation thesis presupposes that there is no conceptually necessary connection between law and morality, between what the law commands and what justice requires, or between the law as it is and the law as it ought to be. The great legal positivist Hans Kelsen captured this in the statement, 'Thus, the content of the law can be anything whatsoever.'[2]

In the positivistic concept of law, then, there are only two defining elements: that of issuance in accordance with the system, or authoritative issuance,[3] and that of social efficacy.

---

[1] A single example: To this day, where a 'law' is understood to be legally valid, different answers are still given to the question Alcibiades puts to Pericles in Xenophon's portrayal. 'Then if a despot, being the ruling power in the state, enacts what the citizens are to do, is this, too, a law?' Xenophon, *Memorabilia*, bk. I, ch. 2, paras. 40–6, 44, trans. Amy L. Bonnette (Ithaca, NY: Cornell University Press, 1994), 13–14, 13 (trans. altered).

[2] Kelsen, *PTL* § 34(c) (p. 198) (trans. altered); see also Kelsen, *LT* § 28 (at p. 56).

[3] The expressions 'issuance in accordance with the system' ('*ordnungs-gemäße Gesetztheit*') and 'authoritative issuance' ('*autoritative Gesetztheit*') can but need not be used synonymously. They are used synonymously when they refer in the same way to norms that establish the competence to issue norms, that is, when they specify who is empowered to issue norms and in what way one is so empowered. In specifying the criteria for issuance in

The numerous variations of legal positivism[4] stem from different interpretations and assessments of these two defining elements.[5] Common to all of the variations is the notion that what law is depends solely on what has been issued and/or is efficacious. Correctness of content—however achieved—counts for nothing.

By contrast to the positivistic theories, all non-positivistic theories defend the *connection thesis*, which says that the concept of law is to be defined such that moral elements are included. No serious non-positivist is thereby excluding from the concept of law either the element of authoritative issuance or the element of social efficacy. Rather, what distinguishes the non-positivist from the positivist is the view that the concept of law is to be defined such that, alongside these fact-oriented properties, moral elements are also included. Here, too, very different interpretations and assessments are possible.

accordance with the system, then, these norms establish norm-issuing authority. Given this premiss, what is issued in accordance with the system is authoritatively issued, and vice versa. The two expressions are not used synonymously when 'issuance in accordance with the system' refers solely to competence norms, while 'authoritative issuance' refers solely or also to the actual power to issue norms. It suffices here simply to point out these variations in meaning. Since the power factor as an aspect of effectiveness can be classified under social efficacy, the two expressions for issuance will be used synonymously in what follows. (The original text of this footnote has been modified by the author.)

[4] See Walter Ott, *Der Rechtspositivismus*, 2nd edn. (Berlin: Duncker & Humblot, 1992), at 32–116.

[5] See Ralf Dreier, 'Der Begriff des Rechts', in Dreier, *Recht—Staat—Vernunft* (Frankfurt: Suhrkamp, 1991), 95–119, at 96.

2. The Practical Significance of the Debate

The debate surrounding the concept of law is a debate about what law is. Every jurist has a more or less clear idea here that is expressed in his or her work in the law. The concept of law underlying the jurist's endeavour is generally presupposed as self-evident, and even where it is less obvious, indulging in conceptual speculation on the law is regarded as a waste of time in the usual run of cases. Unusual, non-standard cases are a different matter, forcing the underlying concept of law to the fore as a pressing problem. The point is illustrated with the help of two decisions of the Federal Constitutional Court of Germany.

A. STATUTORY INJUSTICE

The first example, a decision of 1968 on citizenship, concerns the problem of statutory injustice. Section 2 of the Eleventh Ordinance (hereafter 'Ordinance 11'), 25 November 1941, issued pursuant to the Statute on Reich Citizenship of 15 September 1935,[6] stripped emigrant Jews of German citizenship on grounds of race. The Federal Constitutional Court was to decide whether, according to this directive, a Jewish lawyer had forfeited German citizenship by emigrating to Amsterdam shortly before the outbreak of the Second World War. He had been deported from Amsterdam in 1942, and since it was not known what had become of him,

---

[6] See respectively *RGBl* I (1941), at 722, and *RGBl* I (1935), at 1146.

he was presumed dead, ruling out the possibility of a restoration of German citizenship in accordance with art. 116, para. 2, of the post-war Basic Law[7] or Constitution of the Federal Republic of Germany.

The Federal Constitutional Court reached the conclusion that the lawyer never lost his German citizenship because Ordinance 11, pursuant to the Statute on Reich Citizenship, was null and void, that is, invalid from the outset. The Court argues as follows:

Law and justice are not left to the discretion of the lawmaker. The idea that a 'constitutional framer can arrange everything as he pleases would mean reverting to a mental posture of value-free statutory positivism that has long since been obsolete in legal science and practice. Precisely the period of the National Socialist regime in Germany has taught that lawlessness [*Unrecht*] can issue even from the lawmaker.'[8] Therefore, the Federal Constitutional Court has affirmed the possibility of revoking the legal validity of National Socialist 'legal' provisions when they conflict with fundamental principles of justice so evidently that the judge who elected to apply them or to acknowledge their legal consequences would be administering lawlessness [*Unrecht*] rather than law.[9]

Ordinance 11 violated these fundamental principles. Its conflict with justice reached such an intolerable degree that the Ordinance must be held to be null and void, that is, invalid from the outset.[10] Moreover, the Ordinance did not become efficacious in virtue of having been observed over a number of years or because some

---

[7] *GG* art. 116, para. 2: 'Former German citizens who, between 30 January 1933 and 8 May 1945, were deprived of their citizenship on political, racial, or religious grounds, and their descendants, shall be regranted German citizenship on application. They shall be considered as not having been deprived of their German citizenship if they established their domicile (*Wohnsitz*) in Germany after 8 May 1945 and have not expressed a contrary intention' (trans. altered).

[8] *BVerfGE* 3 (1954), 225, at 232 (citation in the Court's opinion).

[9] ibid. 58, at 119; ibid. 6 (1957), 132, at 198 (citation in the Court's opinion).

[10] See *BGH*, in *RzW* (1962), 563; *BGHZ* 9 (1953), 33, at 44; ibid. 10 (1953), 340, at 342; ibid. 16 (1955), 350, at 354; ibid. 26 (1958), 91, at 93 (citation in the Court's opinion).

persons subject to 'denaturalization' had at the time come to terms or even concurred with National Socialist measures in particular cases. Duly enacted lawlessness that is obviously in violation of the constituting basic principles of the law does not become law in virtue of having been applied and obeyed.[11]

This is a classic non-positivistic argument. An authoritatively issued norm, socially efficacious from the time of issuance, is denied validity or—the decision is ambiguous here—legal character because it violates suprastatutory law.

One can ask whether this argument was altogether necessary in the decision on citizenship. The Court could have sought to substantiate its finding solely with the argument that *present* recognition of the legal efficacy of this deprivation of citizenship violates both the general equality provision of art. 3, para. 1, of the Basic Law[12] as well as the prohibitions of discrimination found in art. 3, para. 3.[13] This possible tack does diminish the weight but not the general significance accorded the non-positivistic argument in the citizenship case decided here. Not in every case involving evaluation of the legal consequences of a rogue regime (*Unrechtsregime*) are there comparable constitutional safeguards. Moreover, there are cases that turn on whether or not a norm was null and void, that is, invalid from the outset, a finding that cannot stem from a later constitution. One thinks, for example, of authoritatively issued and socially efficacious norms of a rogue regime that command or permit persecution measures contrary to human rights.[14] The question of whether persons who acted in accordance with these norms can be punished after the downfall of the rogue regime depends largely—where no retroactive statute is enacted—on whether or not these norms were null and void, that is, invalid from the outset.

---

[11] *BVerfGE* 23 (1968), 98, at 106.

[12] *GG* art. 3, para. 1: 'All persons are equal before the law.'

[13] *GG* art. 3, para. 3: 'No one may be disadvantaged or favoured because of his sex, his parentage, his race, his language, his homeland and origin, his faith, or his religious or political opinions.'

[14] *BGHSt* 2 (1952), 173, at 174–7.

B. Judicial Development of the Law

The second example, a decision of 1973 on judicial development of the law, concerns the permissibility of law development
by judges that is contrary to the literal reading of a statute—
the permissibility, in other words, of a *contra legem*[15] decision.
According to section 253 of the German Civil Code, monetary
compensation for non-material harm is precluded except in
the narrowly defined cases provided by statute. The Federal
Supreme Court has not adhered to this regulation, having
granted, since 1958, monetary compensation in a great many
cases involving major violations of the right to personal priv-
acy. The case at issue concerned a weekly magazine that had
published a completely fabricated interview about private
matters that Princess Soraya, the ex-wife of the last Shah of
Iran, sought to have protected. The Federal Supreme Court
awarded Princess Soraya damages in the amount of 15,000
German marks, at odds with the literal reading of section 253
of the Civil Code, permitting *solatium*, or damages for non-
material harm, 'only in those cases specified by statute'. The
case of Princess Soraya clearly was not one of these cases. The
Federal Constitutional Court upheld the decision of the Federal Supreme Court. A pivotal part of its argument runs as
follows:

The traditional view that the judge is bound by the statute—a
significant component of the principle of the separation of powers
and thereby of the *Rechtsstaat* or rule of law—has been modified at
least in its formulation in the Basic Law to read that the judiciary is
bound by 'statute and law' ['*Gesetz und Recht*'].[16] The received
opinion is that with this formulation, a narrow statutory positivism
is being rejected. The wording supports the sense that statute and
law do in fact generally coincide, but not necessarily and always.
The law is not identical with the totality of written statutes.

---

[15] Literally 'contrary to law'.

[16] *GG* art. 20, para. 3 (citation in the Court's opinion): 'Legislation is
subject to the constitutional order; the executive and the judiciary are
bound by statute and law' (trans. altered).

As against the express directives of state authorities, there can be in some circumstances a greater law that has its source in the constitutional legal system as a totality of meaning and that may function as a corrective vis-à-vis the written statute; to discover this law and to put it into practice in decisions is the task of the judiciary.[17]

The decision of the Federal Constitutional Court is controversial. The charge against the Court is that civil courts were not themselves permitted to decide on a restriction of the text of section 253 of the Civil Code; rather, in accordance with concrete judicial review as provided by art. 100, para. 1, of the Basic Law,[18] they would have had to request a decision of the Federal Constitutional Court as to whether section 253 conforms to the constitution.[19] The merits of this objection turn,

---

[17] *BVerfGE* 34 (1973), 269, 286–7. While the Federal Constitutional Court, in later decisions, has on several occasions exercised greater caution in commenting on judicial law development *contra legem* or contrary to the literal reading of the statute, it has maintained the fundamental permissibility of such development; see *BVerfGE* 35 (1974), 263, at 278–80; ibid. 37 (1975), 67, at 81; ibid. 38 (1975), 386, at 396–7; ibid. 49 (1979), 304, at 318–22; ibid. 65 (1984), 182, at 190–5; ibid. 71 (1986), 354, at 362–3; ibid. 82 (1991), 6, at 11–15.

[18] *GG* art. 100, para. 1: 'If a court considers that a statute on whose validity the court's decision depends is unconstitutional, the proceedings shall be stayed, and a decision shall be obtained from the *Land* court with jurisdiction over constitutional disputes when the constitution of a *Land* is held to be violated, or from the Federal Constitutional Court when this Basic Law is held to be violated. This shall also apply when the Basic Law is held to be violated by *Land* law or where a *Land* statute is held to be incompatible with a federal statute.'

[19] See Hans-Joachim Koch and Helmut Rüßmann, *Juristische Begründungslehre* (Munich: C. H. Beck, 1982), at 255; see also Friedrich Müller, '*Richterrecht*' (Berlin: Duncker & Humblot, 1986), at 69–70. § 253 *BGB* is pre-constitutional law. According to the opinions of the Federal Constitutional Court, § 253 *BGB*, as pre-constitutional law, can be subjected to concrete judicial review as provided by art. 100, para. 1, of the Basic Law only if the federal legislator has 'incorporated it into his legislative policy', *BVerfGE* 64 (1984), 217, at 220. Where that is not the case, the civil courts would have been able to hold § 253 *BGB* unconstitutional in part for violating *GG* art. 2, para. 1, in connection with *GG* art. 1, para. 1. The obstacle presented by the literal reading of § 253 *BGB* would then have been eliminated for these courts.

first, on whether or not the non-positivistic interpretation of the clause 'statute and law' in art. 20, para. 3, of the Basic Law is correct and, second, on the question of how, if that interpretation is correct, the relation between art. 20, para. 3, and art. 100, para. 1, of the Basic Law is to be defined. Only the first of these is of interest here. The significance of the statement, 'The law is not identical with the totality of written statutes', is preserved even if one holds that, because of the procedure provided in the German legal system by art. 100, para. 1, of the Basic Law, *contra legem* decisions are generally impermissible. The problem of the *contra legem* decision arises in every legal system, although not every legal system has a procedure for concrete judicial review like that provided by art. 100, para. 1, of the Basic Law. What is more important still, far beyond the realm of *contra legem* decisions, is that this statement has significance in every doubtful case. A doubtful case is, say, when the statute to be applied is indeterminate and the rules of legal method do not lead definitively to precisely one result. Whoever identifies the law with the written statute, that is, whoever endorses the thesis of statutory positivism,[20] must say that in doubtful cases the decision is determined by extra-legal factors. The position of the non-positivist is altogether different. For the non-positivist, who does not identify the law with the statute, the decision can be determined by the law even if it is not definitively prescribed by the statute. To be sure, differing views of what law is need not lead to different results—but they can.

---

[20] Only one variation of legal positivism, namely, statutory positivism, is under consideration here. The argument can easily be extended, however, to other species of positivism.

II

The Concept of Law

1. Central Elements

The question is this: Which concept of law is correct or adequate? An answer to the question turns on the relation of three elements to one another—authoritative *issuance*, social *efficacy*, and *correctness* of content. Altogether different concepts of law emerge according to how the relative significance of these elements is assessed. Attaching no significance whatsoever to authoritative issuance and social efficacy, focusing exclusively on correctness of content, one arrives at a concept of law purely reflective of natural law or the law of reason. One arrives at a purely positivistic concept of law by ruling out correctness of content altogether and staking everything on authoritative issuance and/or social efficacy. Between these extremes, many intermediate forms are possible.

The tripartite division indicates that positivism has two defining elements. A positivist must exclude the element of correctness of content, but then can define in many different ways the relation between the elements of authoritative issuance and social efficacy, giving rise to numerous variations of legal positivism. I look first at the differing versions and then criticize positivistic concepts of law as inadequate.

2. *Positivistic Concepts of Law*

Not only is it possible to combine the elements of social efficacy and authoritative issuance in different ways, it is possible to interpret them very differently, too. Because of this, the variety of positivistic concepts of law is wellnigh unlimited. These can be divided into two main groups: concepts of law that are primarily oriented toward efficacy and those that are primarily oriented toward issuance. The qualifier 'primarily' should make it clear that, as a rule, a given orientation represents simply the main focus, meaning that the other element is not being altogether excluded.

A. PRIMARILY ORIENTED TOWARD EFFICACY

Definitions of law that are oriented toward efficacy are usually found in the realm of sociological and realist legal theories. What distinguishes one definition from another is whether the focus is on the external or the internal aspect of a norm or a system of norms. Here too, in most cases, the distinction reflects relative significance, not a strict dichotomy. And, in addition, there are frequently combinations of external and internal aspects.[21]

(i) External Aspect

The external aspect of a norm consists in the regularity of compliance with the norm and/or the imposition of a sanction

---

[21] An example of a combination of the external with the internal aspect is found in Alf Ross, *Of Law and Justice*, trans. Margaret Dutton (London: Stevens & Sons, 1974), at 73–4.

for non-compliance. What counts is observable behaviour, even that requiring interpretation, and the main thrust of sociological definitions of law focuses there. Examples are the definitions of Max Weber and Theodor Geiger. Weber writes:

A system is to be called... *law* if it is externally guaranteed by the possibility of (physical or psychic) *coercion* through action aimed at enforcing compliance or punishing violation, the action of a *staff* of persons *expressly* geared to this task.[22]

Geiger's definition reads:

What law is, that is, the content that it seems to me practical to characterize with the word 'law', has already been explained in great detail: the social system of a centrally organized, broadly inclusive community, provided this system is based on a sanction-apparatus implemented monopolistically by particular organs.[23]

Efficacy-oriented concepts of law that focus on the external aspect are also found in legal philosophy, especially in pragmatic instrumentalism or legal realism. A famous example is the predictive definition of Oliver Wendell Holmes:

The prophecies of what the courts will do in fact, and nothing more pretentious, are what I mean by the law.[24]

---

[22] Max Weber, *Law in Economy and Society*, trans. Max Rheinstein, in Weber, *Economy and Society* (1st pub. 1922), ed. Guenther Roth and Claus Wittich (Berkeley and Los Angeles: University of California Press, 1978), pt. I, ch. 1, sect. 6 (p. 34) (emphasis in original) (trans. altered). In its details, Max Weber's sociological concept of law is far more complex than the quotation would suggest. Here, however, as with the other examples of definitions, we are concerned simply with the basic idea. For a more detailed account of Weber's concept of law, see Fritz Loos, *Zur Wert- und Rechtslehre Max Webers* (Tübingen: J. C. B. Mohr, 1970), at 93–112.

[23] Theodor Geiger, *Vorstudien zu einer Soziologie des Rechts* (1st pub. 1947), 4th edn., ed. Manfred Rehbinder (Berlin: Duncker & Humblot, 1987), 297.

[24] Oliver Wendell Holmes, 'The Path of the Law', *Harvard Law Review*, 10 (1896–7), 457–78, at 461, repr. in Holmes, *Collected Legal Papers* (New York: Harcourt, Brace and Howe, 1920), 167–202, at 173. See Robert S. Summers, *Instrumentalism and American Legal Theory* (Ithaca, NY: Cornell University Press, 1982), at 116–35.

Definitions of this kind are addressed primarily to the perspective of the lawyer.

(ii) Internal Aspect

The internal aspect of a norm consists in the motivation—however generated—for compliance with the norm and/or for application of the norm. What counts are psychic dispositions, and one example of a definition with that focus is Ernst Rudolf Bierling's, where the concept of recognition plays a central role:

> Law in the juridical sense is generally everything that human beings who live together in some community or another mutually recognize as norm and rule of their life together.[25]

Niklas Luhmann provides another variant of a legal definition in which an essential role is played by the internal aspect, here in the form of a normative expectation of behaviour:

> We can now define law as structure of a social system, a structure based on the congruent generalization of normative expectations of behaviour.[26]

B. PRIMARILY ORIENTED TOWARD ISSUANCE

Concepts of law that are oriented toward issuance are usually found in analytical legal theory, that is, in that branch of legal theory where the first concern is the logical or conceptual analysis of the jurist's participation in the law. While it is the observer's perspective that is dominant in concepts of law oriented toward efficacy, it is the participant's perspec-

---

[25] Bierling, Ernst Rudolf, *Juristische Prinzipienlehre*, vol. 1 (Freiburg i. Br. and Leipzig: J. C. B. Mohr, 1894, repr. Aalen: Scientia, 1979), 19.

[26] Niklas Luhmann, *A Sociological Theory of Law*, trans. Elizabeth King and Martin Albrow (London: Routledge & Kegan Paul, 1985), 82 (emphasis omitted) (trans. altered).

tive—in particular, the judge's—that is foremost in concepts of law oriented toward issuance.

A classic example of a concept of law oriented toward issuance is found in the work of John Austin. According to Austin, the law is composed of commands:

Every law or rule ... is a command.[27]

A command is defined as being armed with a sanction:

A command is distinguished from other significations of desire, not by the style in which the desire is signified, but by the power and the purpose of the party commanding to inflict an evil or pain in case the desire be disregarded.[28]

Not every command, but, rather, only the command of a politically superior authority is law:

Of the laws or rules set by men to men, some are established by political superiors, sovereign and subject: by persons exercising supreme and subordinate government, in independent nations, or independent political societies ... To the aggregate of the rules thus established, or to some aggregate forming a portion of that aggregate, the term law, as used simply and strictly, is exclusively applied.[29]

Summarizing, one can say that Austin defines the law as the totality of a sovereign's commands armed with sanctions. While a stronger orientation toward issuance is scarcely possible, elements of efficacy also play a not unimportant role in Austin's theory. Thus, in defining the sovereign as someone who is customarily obeyed, Austin combines the element of issuance with the element of efficacy:

If a determinate human superior, not in a habit of obedience to a like superior, receive habitual obedience from the bulk of a given society, that determinate superior is sovereign in that society ...[30]

---

[27] Austin, *Province* 13; Austin, *Lectures* vol. 1, 88 (emphasis omitted).
[28] Austin, *Province* 14; Austin, *Lectures* vol. 1, 89.
[29] Austin, *Province* 11; Austin, *Lectures* vol. 1, 86–7 (emphasis omitted).
[30] Austin, *Province* 194; Austin, *Lectures* vol. 1, 221 (emphasis omitted).

The most significant twentieth-century representatives of issuance-oriented legal positivism are Hans Kelsen and H. L. A. Hart. Kelsen defines the law as a 'normative coercive order'[31] whose validity rests on a presupposed basic norm

> according to which one ought to comply with a constitution actually issued and by and large efficacious, and therefore ought also to comply with norms actually issued in accordance with this constitution and themselves by and large efficacious.[32]

The status of Kelsen's basic norm will be considered below.[33] Here it suffices to note that the basic norm is an altogether content-neutral norm that is only imagined or thought, a norm, according to Kelsen, that must be presupposed if one's aim is to interpret a coercive system as a legal system. What is of significance here is simply that Kelsen's definition, while it is indeed primarily oriented toward issuance, also includes the element of efficacy:

> In the basic norm, issuance and efficacy are made a condition for validity—efficacy in the sense that it must be added to issuance so that the legal system as a whole, as well as an individual legal norm, not forfeit its validity.[34]

According to Hart, the law is a system of rules that are identified by appeal to a rule of recognition.[35] While the function of Hart's rule of recognition corresponds to that of Kelsen's basic norm, its status is altogether different, something to which I return below.[36] Its existence is a social fact:

> [T]he rule of recognition exists only as a complex, but normally concordant, practice of the courts, officials, and private persons in identifying the law by reference to certain criteria. Its existence is a matter of fact.[37]

---

[31] See Kelsen, *PTL*, at § 6(c) (pp. 44–50).
[32] See ibid. § 34(g) (at p. 212) (trans. altered).
[33] See below, this text, at 96–116.
[34] Kelsen, *PTL* § 34(g) (at p. 212) (trans. altered).
[35] (This sentence of the original text has been modified by the author.)
[36] See below, this text, at 121–3.
[37] Hart, *CL* 107, 2nd edn. 110.

Hart formulates a pivotal point of the rule of recognition for the English legal system: '[W]hat the Queen in Parliament enacts is law.'[38]

[38] Hart, *CL* 104, 2nd edn. 107.

3. Critique of Positivistic Concepts of Law

This brief look at positivistic concepts of law shows that very different positions are represented within the field known as legal positivism. The only thing common to all of them is the thesis of the separation of law and morality. If the positivistic separation thesis were certainly correct, analysis of the concept of law could be completely confined to the questions of what the best interpretation is of the elements of efficacy and issuance and how the relation between the two elements is best understood. The Federal Constitutional Court decisions sketched above, however, show that the separation thesis can at least be regarded as less than obvious. So the question becomes whether a positivistic concept of law as such is adequate in the first place, and that depends on whether it is the separation thesis or the connection thesis that is correct.

A. Separation Thesis and Connection Thesis

The separation thesis and the connection thesis tell us how the concept of law is to be defined. They formulate the result of a line of reasoning without giving voice to the arguments behind it. The supporting arguments can be divided into two groups: analytical and normative.[39]

---

[39] One might think of a third group of arguments, namely, empirical arguments. On closer inspection, however, one sees that, where the concept of law is being defined in terms of either the separation thesis or the connection thesis, empirical arguments become components of analytical or normative arguments. It is an empirical thesis that a legal system that

The most important *analytical* argument for the positivistic separation thesis is that there is no conceptually necessary connection between law and morality. Every positivist must defend this thesis, for if it is granted that a conceptually necessary connection between law and morality does exist, then it can no longer be said that the definition of law is to exclude moral elements. By contrast, the non-positivist is free in arguing at the analytical level. He can either claim a conceptually necessary connection or not. If he succeeds in spelling out a conceptually necessary connection, he has settled the debate in his favour. If he fails in spelling out or does not claim a conceptually necessary connection, he has not yet lost the debate. He can appeal to normative arguments in attempting to support his thesis that the definition of the concept of law is to incorporate moral elements.

It is a *normative* argument that supports the separation thesis or the connection thesis when it is stated that, to attain a certain goal or to comply with a certain norm, it is necessary to exclude or to include moral elements in the concept of law. A separation or a connection justified in this way may be called 'normatively necessary'.[40] It is a normative argument, for example, when it is stated that only the separation thesis

protects neither the life nor the liberty nor the property of any legal subject has no prospect of long-term validity. But the protection of life, liberty, and property is also a moral requirement. Thus it can be said that the satisfaction of certain minimum moral requirements is factually necessary for the long-term validity of a legal system. The empirical argument leads to precisely this point and no further. The bridge to the concept of law is inserted into an analytical argument that says that, for conceptual reasons, only systems having long-term validity are legal systems. By contrast, there is an insertion into a normative argument when, for example, the empirical thesis that certain goals like survival can be attained only if the law has a certain content, coupled with the normative premiss that this goal ought to be attained, is adduced as an argument for a certain definition of law.

[40] Normative necessity is strictly to be distinguished from conceptual necessity. That something is normatively necessary means nothing other than that it is commanded. One can, without contradicting oneself, challenge the validity of a command but not the existence of a conceptual necessity. It is clear that only in a broader sense, then, is normative necessity a necessity.

leads to linguistic and conceptual clarity or guarantees legal certainty, or when it is established that the problems of statutory injustice can best be resolved with the help of the connection thesis.

In recent debates about the concept of law, the prevailing view has been that the expression 'law' is so ambiguous, so vague, that nothing in the debate about legal positivism can be settled by means of conceptual analysis,[41] that what is at stake here is simply 'a normative determination, a definitional postulate'.[42] This kind of concept formation can, by definition, only be justified by normative arguments or considerations of expediency, a thesis presupposing the thesis that a connection between law and morality is neither conceptually impossible nor conceptually necessary. The first part of this presupposed thesis is correct, that is, the claim that a connection between law and morality is not conceptually impossible. In some contexts there is no contradiction in a sentence like: 'The norm N is authoritatively issued and socially efficacious but not law, for it violates fundamental principles.' Such a sentence would have to be contradictory, however, if a connection between law and morality were conceptually impossible. The second part of the thesis, on the other hand, is doubtful—that is, the claim that there is no conceptually necessary connection between law and morality. Indeed, in what follows, just such a connection will be shown to exist. And if this showing is successful, then the prevailing view is incorrect, the view, namely, that the debate surrounding the concept of law turns exclusively on an expediential decision that can only be justified by normative arguments. I do not mean to suggest that in the discussion on the concept of law, normative considerations have no role to play. The conceptual argument will prove to be limited both in range and in force; and beyond that range, as well as to strengthen the conceptual argument, normative arguments are necessary.

[41] See Ott, *Der Rechtspositivismus* (n. 4 above), at 142–53.
[42] Hoerster, *VR* 2481.

The thesis runs: first, there is a conceptually necessary connection between law and morality, and, second, there are normative arguments for including moral elements in the concept of law, arguments that in part strengthen and in part go beyond the conceptually necessary connection. In short, there are conceptually necessary as well as normatively necessary connections between law and morality.

B. A CONCEPTUAL FRAMEWORK

The thesis that there are conceptually necessary as well as normatively necessary connections between law and morality will be substantiated within a conceptual framework consisting of five distinctions.[43]

(i) Concepts of Law Omitting Validity and Embracing Validity

The first distinction is between concepts of law that *omit* validity and those that *embrace* validity. The former is a concept of law that does not include the concept of validity, the latter, a concept of law that does.[44] It is easy to see that there is occasion for making this distinction. One can say without contradiction, '*N* is a legal norm, but *N* is not (is no longer, is not yet) valid.' And, imagining an ideal legal system, one can remark without contradiction, 'This legal system will never be valid.' Conversely, in appealing to valid law, one need not speak of validity; one can simply say, 'This is required by law.' Thus, both are clearly possible: a concept of law that includes the concept of validity, as well as a concept of law that does not include the concept of validity.

---

[43] See Robert Alexy, 'On Necessary Relations between Law and Morality', *Ratio Juris*, 2 (1989), 167–83.

[44] See Hermann Kantorowicz, *The Definition of Law*, ed. A. H. Campbell, with an introduction by A. L. Goodhart (Cambridge: Cambridge University Press, 1958), at 16–20.

For the discussion of positivism, it is well to select a concept of law that includes the concept of validity. What can be avoided thereby is trivializing the problem by first ignoring the dimension of validity and defining the law as a class of norms, say, for external behaviour,[45] in order to argue, then, that because it is possible to imagine the content of norms for external behaviour being anything whatsoever, there can be no conceptually necessary connection between law and morality. Incorporating into the concept of law the concept of validity means including in the concept of law the institutional context of lawmaking, law application, and law enforcement, a context that can be of significance on the question of a conceptually necessary connection between law and morality.

(ii) Legal Systems as Systems of Norms and as Systems of Procedures

The second distinction is between the legal system as a system of norms and the legal system as a system of procedures.[46] As a system of *procedures*, the legal system is a system of processes or actions based on and governed by rules, actions by means of which norms are issued, justified, interpreted, applied, and enforced. As a system of *norms*, the legal system is a system of results or products of norm-creating procedures, whatever the origin or character of these procedures. One can say that to regard the legal system as a system of

[45] See Ralf Dreier, 'Neues Naturrecht oder Rechtspositivismus?' *Rechtstheorie*, 18 (1987), 368–85, at 374–5.

[46] On the legal system as a system of procedures, see Robert Alexy, 'Die Idee einer prozeduralen Theorie der juristischen Argumentation', in *MEA* 177–88, at 185–8, repr. in Alexy, *Recht, Vernunft, Diskurs. Studien zur Rechtsphilosophie* (Frankfurt: Suhrkamp, 1995), 94–108, at 104–8. Lon L. Fuller's distinction between 'the purposive effort that goes into the making of law and the law that in fact emerges from that effort', Fuller, *The Morality of Law*, rev. edn. (New Haven: Yale University Press, 1969), 193, may well approach the distinction between norm and procedure introduced here.

norms is to refer to its external side, whereas to regard it as a system of procedures is to refer to its internal side.

(iii) Observer's and Participant's Perspectives

The third distinction is between the observer's perspective and the participant's perspective. This dichotomy is ambiguous, and the interpretation here is as follows. The *participant's perspective* is adopted by one who, within a legal system, participates in disputation about what is commanded, forbidden, and permitted in this legal system and to what end this legal system confers power. At the centre of the participant's perspective stands the judge. When other participants—say, legal scholars, attorneys, or interested citizens—adduce arguments for or against certain contents of the legal system, they refer in the end to how a judge would have to decide if he wanted to decide correctly. The *observer's perspective* is adopted by one who asks not what the correct decision is in a certain legal system, but, rather, how decisions are actually made in a certain legal system. An example of this kind of observer is Norbert Hoerster's white American, who, wanting to travel with his African-American wife in South Africa, where apartheid laws prevailed at the time, reflected on legal particulars of his trip.[47]

The distinction between the participant's perspective and the observer's perspective is related to H. L. A. Hart's distinction between internal and external points of view.[48] Correspondence in every respect, however, is out of the question, if for no other reason than the ambiguity of Hart's distinction.[49] Therefore, this proviso: Whenever I speak of an internal and an external standpoint without further elucidation, I mean precisely what I have defined above as the participant's perspective and the observer's perspective.

[47] Hoerster, *VR* 2481.
[48] Hart, *CL* 86–7, 2nd edn. 88–90.
[49] See Neil MacCormick, *Legal Reasoning and Legal Theory* (Oxford: Clarendon Press, 1978), at 275–92.

(iv) Classifying and Qualifying Connections

The fourth distinction refers to two different kinds of connection between law and morality. I shall call the first 'classifying', the second 'qualifying'. A *classifying* connection is reflected in the claim that norms or systems of norms that do not meet a certain moral criterion are, for either conceptual or normative reasons, not legal norms or legal systems. A *qualifying* connection is reflected in the claim that norms or systems of norms that do not meet a certain moral criterion can indeed be legal norms or legal systems, but, for either conceptual or normative reasons, are legally defective legal norms or legal systems. What is crucial is that the asserted defect is a legal defect and not simply a moral defect. Arguments addressed to qualifying connections are based on the assumption that necessarily legal ideals are contained within the reality of a legal system. Thus, instead of a 'qualifying' connection, one could also speak of an 'ideal' connection.

(v) Conceptually Necessary and Normatively
    Necessary Connections

In addition to these four distinctions—between a concept of law that omits validity and one that embraces validity, between norm and procedure, between observer and participant, and between classifying and qualifying connections—there is the distinction, introduced above, between a *conceptually necessary* and a *normatively necessary connection*. With these five distinctions, the conceptual framework is complete.

(vi) Combinations

The framework makes it clear that very different meanings can be attached to the thesis that a necessary connection exists between law and morality. Within the framework, there are thirty-two possible combinations of the components of the five distinctions. For each combination, both the thesis that a necessary connection exists, as well as the thesis that a necessary connection does not exist, can be formulated. There emerge, then, sixty-four theses altogether. Now, among these, there are certainly a number of implicative relations, which is to say that the truth or falsity of some of the theses implies the truth or falsity of others. And it may be that some combinations are conceptually impossible. That changes nothing, however, in the fundamental insight that a multitude of different claims are made in the debate about necessary connections between law and morality. One explanation for the inconclusiveness of this debate may be that the respective debaters often fail to recognize that the thesis they are defending is altogether different in kind from the thesis they are attacking, with the result that they are talking at cross purposes with one another. This explanation seems even more plausible when one considers that alongside the five distinctions in play here, further distinctions are imaginable, so that the number of possible theses could swell well beyond sixty-four.

In one respect, the large number of possible theses has already been reduced here, namely, in that our point of departure is a concept of law that includes the concept of validity. Simplifying things further is our emphasis on one distinction, the distinction between the observer's perspective or external standpoint and the participant's perspective or internal standpoint. It is within the framework of this dichotomy that the other distinctions come into play. The question, then, is whether the separation thesis or the connection thesis is correct from the observer's perspective or from the participant's perspective.

C. The Observer's Perspective

The problem of legal positivism is discussed for the most part as the problem of a classifying connection between law and morality. One asks whether contravention of some moral criterion or another exacts from the norms of a system of norms the character of legal norms, or from the whole system of norms the character of a legal system. If one aims to answer this question in the affirmative, one must show that legal character is forfeited when norms or systems of norms cross a certain threshold of injustice (*Unrecht*). It is precisely this thesis that I shall call the 'argument from injustice', the thesis, namely, of forfeiting legal character by crossing a certain threshold of injustice, however that threshold is to be determined.[50] The argument from injustice is nothing other than the connection thesis focused on a classifying connection. It should be asked here, first of all, whether the connection thesis in the form of the argument from injustice is correct from the observer's perspective, an enquiry in which individual norms of a legal system are to be distinguished from the legal system as a whole.

(i) Individual Norms

Probably the best-known version of the argument from injustice applied to individual norms stems from Gustav Radbruch, whose famous formula reads:

The conflict between justice and legal certainty may well be resolved in this way: The positive law, secured by legislation and power, takes precedence even when its content is unjust and inexpedient, unless the conflict between statute and justice reaches such an intolerable degree that the statute, as 'lawless law', must yield to justice.[51]

This formula is the basis for the decision on citizenship set out above,[52] as well as for a number of other decisions of the

---

[50] Dreier, 'Der Begriff des Rechts' (n. 5 above), 99. Other names are the argument from tyranny, the *lex corrupta* argument, the argument from perversion of law, the argument from totalitarianism.

[51] Radbruch, *GUR* 107, *RGA 3* 89.

[52] *BVerfGE* 23 (1968), 98, at 106. See above, this text, at 5–7.

Federal Constitutional Court and the Federal Supreme Court of Germany.[53] Is Radbruch's formula acceptable from the standpoint of an observer? Once again, our example is Ordinance 11 of 25 November 1941, by means of which emigrant Jews were stripped of German citizenship on grounds of race. In the related decision discussed above, the Federal Constitutional Court appealed to Radbruch's formula in holding Ordinance 11 to be null and void. This represents the participant's perspective. How would the case of the denaturalized Jew, call him '*A*', be described by a contemporary observer of the National Socialist legal system, say, a jurist from abroad who is writing a report for a law journal back home on the legal system of National Socialism? Everyone back home would understand, without further elucidation, the jurist's statement,

(1) *A* has been deprived of citizenship according to German law.

That is not the case with the statement,

(2) *A* has not been deprived of citizenship according to German law.

If no further information is given, this statement either informs incorrectly or creates confusion.

This shows that from the external standpoint of the observer, the inclusion of moral elements in the concept of law is at any rate not conceptually necessary. Rather, there is occasion to ask whether, from this standpoint, such an inclusion is conceptually impossible. Assume that the report of our observer contains the following statement:

(3) *A* has not been deprived of citizenship according to German law, although all German courts and officials

---

[53] See *BVerfGE* 3 (1954), 58, at 119; ibid. 225, at 233; ibid. 6 (1957), 132, at 198; ibid. 309, at 332; ibid. 389, at 414–15; ibid. 54 (1981), 53, at 67–8; *BGHZ* 3 (1951), 94, at 107; ibid. 23 (1957), 175, at 181; *BGHSt* 2 (1952), 173, at 177; ibid. 234, at 238–9; ibid. 3 (1953), 357, at 362–3.

treat *A* as denaturalized and support their action by appeal to the literal reading of a norm authoritatively issued in accordance with the criteria for validity that are part of the legal system efficacious in Germany.

This statement, as the statement of an observer, contains a contradiction. From the standpoint of an observer, the law includes whatever courts and officials do when they support their action by appeal to the literal reading of norms authoritatively issued in accordance with the criteria for validity that are part of the currently efficacious legal system. Thus it is clear that in the observer's perspective, the expression 'law' can be used in such a way that, as applied to individual norms, not only is a classifying inclusion of moral elements in the concept of law not conceptually necessary, it is also conceptually impossible. There is no adequate rejoinder here in countering that our observer can conclude his report straightaway by putting the open question,

(4) *A* has been authoritatively deprived of citizenship in accordance with the criteria valid in Germany, and the denaturalization is socially efficacious as well, but is it law?

With this question, the position of the observer is abandoned and that of the critic is adopted, a shift lending another meaning to the expression 'law'.[54] For the record then: From the perspective of an observer, Radbruch's connection thesis cannot be supported by appeal to a conceptually necessary connection between law and morality.

In addition to this conceptual or analytical argument, there is, by way of an expediential consideration, a normative argument. Norbert Hoerster has claimed, first, that there is a need for a value-neutral designation for authoritatively issued and

---

[54] The change in meaning also applies to what is conceptually necessary or analytically true. On the thesis that what is conceptually necessary or analytically true is dependent on usage, see D. W. Hamlyn, 'Analytic and Synthetic Statements', in *The Encyclopedia of Philosophy*, ed. Paul Edwards (New York: Macmillan and Free Press, 1967), vol. 1, 105–9, at 108.

socially efficacious norms like Ordinance 11 discussed above, and, second, that there is no useful alternative to the expression 'law'.[55] In terms of the observer's perspective, I agree with this.[56] Thus, analytical as well as normative considerations lead to the conclusion that, from the standpoint of an observer who looks at individual norms and enquires into a classifying connection, the positivistic separation thesis is correct. Radbruch's argument from injustice is not acceptable from this standpoint.

(ii) Legal Systems

What applies to an individual norm need not apply to a legal system as a whole.[57] The question, then, is whether a conceptually necessary connection exists between a legal system as a whole and morality. The question is posed, again, from the standpoint of an observer who enquires into a classifying connection, that is, who wants to know whether the contravention of some moral requirement or another exacts from a system of norms the character of a legal system.

There are two kinds of moral requirement that can be necessarily connected to the legal system: formal and material. Fuller's theory of the internal morality of the law is an example of a theory that claims a necessary connection between formal moral criteria and the legal system. Fuller includes the principles of legality, the generality of the law, promulgation, and the prohibition of retroactive laws.[58] By contrast, the connection is between material moral criteria and the legal system when Otfried Höffe claims that a system

---

[55] Hoerster, *LR* 187.

[56] I do not endorse, however, the more general thesis that what is true of the 'exclusively externally descriptive' standpoint is also correct for all other standpoints, Hoerster, *LR* 187–8. Different concepts of law may well correspond to different standpoints, and that they ought to do so will be shown below.

[57] Hart, *PSLM* 621, repr. Hart, *Essays* 78.

[58] Fuller, *The Morality of Law* (n. 46 above), 46–62.

of norms that does not meet certain fundamental criteria for justice is not a legal system.[59] Höffe determines these fundamental criteria for justice through the principle of distributive advantage, a principle including the principle of collective security, which, *inter alia*, requires that a proscription of murder and manslaughter, as well as of robbery and theft, be addressed to all members of the legal community.[60]

In discussing these kinds of connection, one must clearly distinguish between factual and conceptual connections.[61] In view of the present character of the world and of human beings, it is a simple but important empirical fact that a legal system containing no general norms, or only secret norms, or only retroactive norms, or protecting neither the lives nor the liberty nor the property of its subjects, has no chance of long-term validity and, in this sense, a long-term existence. Rather than pursuing this here, however, our question is whether such a system still falls within the concept of the legal system.

There are two kinds of social order that, independently of whether or not they can show long-term validity, are for conceptual reasons alone not legal systems: senseless, and predatory or rapacious orders. A *senseless* order exists when a group of individuals is ruled such that consistent purposes of the ruler or rulers are not discernible nor is a long-term pursuit of a purpose by the ruled possible. Imagine a large number of people who are subject to armed desperadoes. The subjects have no rights, and among the desperadoes themselves, every exercise of force is allowed. Except for this permissory norm, there is no general norm.[62] The armed

---

[59] Otfried Höffe, *Politische Gerechtigkeit* (Frankfurt: Suhrkamp, 1987), 159, 170.

[60] ibid. 169–71.

[61] Kelsen is aiming at a merely factual connection when he characterizes a 'minimum of collective security' as a 'condition for relatively long-term efficacy' but not as a necessary moral element of the concept of law. Kelsen, *PTL* § 6(c) (p. 48) (trans. altered).

[62] Here Kelsen would not even speak of a 'robber band'. The desperadoes, lacking a proscription of the use of force among themselves, are not a community and therefore not a 'band' either; ibid. § 6(c) (p. 47).

desperadoes issue to their subjects individual commands that are sometimes contradictory, always changing, and sometimes impossible to carry out. If the subjects obey a command, they do so solely out of fear. Such a social order is for conceptual reasons alone not a legal system.

The senseless order becomes a *predatory* or rapacious order if the desperadoes organize themselves into a gang of bandits, which presupposes at the least the introduction among themselves of a command hierarchy and a proscription of the use of force. Assume further that a system of rules for the subjects is decreed that has as its sole purpose permanently maintaining the subjects as suitable objects of exploitation. An extreme example: A primary source of revenue for the bandits is that they regularly kill subjects in order to sell their organs. To have available the healthiest possible victims for this purpose, the bandits forbid smoking, drinking, and all violence among their subjects. These rules establish no rights for the subjects, that is, no obligations on the part of the bandits toward the subjects. The purpose of the exploitation is clear to everyone, the bandits making no effort whatsoever to hush it up. One can quarrel over whether the system of norms prevailing among the bandits themselves is a legal system, but, for conceptual reasons alone, the system as a whole is not.[63] To establish this, we turn now to a third kind of social order.

In the long run, the predatory order proves not to be expedient, so the bandits strive to acquire legitimacy. They develop into governors and thereby transform the predatory order into a *governor system*. They continue to exploit their subjects, but their acts of exploitation proceed according to a rule-driven practice. Everyone is told that this practice is correct because it serves a higher purpose, say, the

---

[63] Applying Augustine's robber-band argument here leads to denial of the legal character of the bandit system. Augustine writes: 'Justice removed, then, what are kingdoms but great bands of robbers? What are bands of robbers themselves but little kingdoms?' Augustine, *The City of God against the Pagans*, trans. R. W. Dyson (Cambridge: Cambridge University Press, 1998), bk. IV, ch. 4 (p. 147).

development of the people. The killing and robbing of governed individuals, acts that in point of fact serve only the exploitative interests of the governors, remain possible at any time. But they are punishable if they are not carried out in a certain form—say, on the strength of the unanimous decision of three members of the group of governors—and if they are not publicly justified by appeal to the higher purpose, the development of the people.

With the move to a governor system, a line is crossed. Although the system is without a doubt unjust in the extreme, its designation as 'legal system' is not conceptually excluded. With that, the question is put: What distinguishes the governor system from the desperado system and the bandit system? The difference is not that here general rules of some kind prevail, for that is already the case in the bandit system. And the difference is not that the governor system is equally advantageous for all, even if only at the minimum level of protecting life, liberty, and property; for in this system, too, killing and robbing the governed remain possible at any time. Rather, the decisive point is that a *claim to correctness* is anchored in the practice of the governor system, a claim that is made to everyone. The claim to correctness is a necessary element of the concept of law. This thesis, called the 'argument from correctness', will be established in the next section. Here, in anticipation of the case to be made, it suffices to say that a system of norms that neither explicitly nor implicitly lays claim to correctness is not a legal system. Every legal system lays claim to correctness.[64] In this respect, the claim to correctness has a classifying significance. An observer can at best in an indirect or extended sense characterize as a 'legal system' a system of norms that neither explicitly nor implicitly makes any claim to correctness.

---

[64] This statement is the point of departure for a rational reconstruction of Radbruch's somewhat opaque statement: 'Law is the reality whose meaning is in serving the legal value, the legal idea.' Radbruch, *LP* § 4 (p. 73) (emphasis omitted) (trans. altered).

This has few practical consequences, for actually existing systems of norms regularly lay claim to correctness, however feebly justified the claim may be. Practically speaking, relevant problems first turn up where the claim to correctness is indeed made but not satisfied. What is significant, however, are the systematic consequences of the claim to correctness; that is, it restricts the positivistic separation thesis a good bit even in the observer's perspective. In this perspective, the separation thesis does in fact count as unrestricted where individual norms are concerned, but with legal systems, the separation thesis—albeit only in extreme and indeed improbable cases—reaches a limit defined by the claim to correctness. This claim moves from the limit in the observer's perspective to the centre in the participant's perspective, thus representing a link between the two.

D. The Participant's Perspective

It has been shown that the positivistic separation thesis is essentially correct from the observer's perspective. Only in the extreme and indeed improbable case of a system of norms that fails even to claim correctness does the separation thesis reach a limit. An altogether different picture emerges if one considers the law from the perspective of a participant, say, a judge. From this perspective, the separation thesis is inadequate, and the connection thesis is correct. In order to establish the point, three arguments shall be considered: the argument from correctness, the argument from injustice, and the argument from principles.

(i) The Argument from Correctness

The argument from correctness is the basis of the other two arguments, that is, the arguments from injustice and from principles. It says that individual legal norms and individual legal decisions as well as legal systems as a whole necessarily lay claim to correctness. A system of norms that neither explicitly nor implicitly makes this claim is not a legal system. In this respect, the claim to correctness has a classifying significance. Legal systems that do indeed make this claim but fail to satisfy it are legally defective legal systems. In this respect, the claim to correctness has a qualifying significance. An exclusively qualifying significance is attached to the claim to correctness of individual legal norms and individual legal decisions. These are legally defective if they do not make the claim to correctness or if they fail to satisfy it.

An objection can be made that the argument from correctness is mistaken in saying that a claim to correctness is necessarily attached to the law. In reply to this objection, two examples might be considered. One example concerns the first article of a new constitution for state X, where the minority oppresses the majority. The minority would like to continue to enjoy the advantages of oppressing the majority, but would like also to be honest. The constitutional assembly therefore adopts as the first article of the constitution the following proposition:

(1) X is a sovereign, federal, and unjust republic.

There is something defective about this constitutional article.[65] The question is where the defect lies.

One might think that the defect is simply that the article is not expedient. After all, the minority wants to preserve the unjust status quo, but its chances of doing so are slim if it does not at least pretend that the status quo is just. There is in fact a *technical defect* of this kind here; still, it does not explain the defectiveness of the article. One might assume that in providing for a republic, the new article scraps a pre-existing monarchy, and one might assume further that the oppressed

---

[65] For a similar argument, see Neil MacCormick, 'Law, Morality and Positivism', *Legal Studies*, 1 (1981), 131–45, at 144, repr. in MacCormick and Ota Weinberger, *An Institutional Theory of Law* (Dordrecht: Reidel, 1986), 127–44, at 141.

majority deeply reveres the former monarch, with the result that the status quo is as threatened by the introduction of the republic as by the characterization of the state as 'unjust'. In this case, the constitutional framer—if the injustice provision were simply a technical defect—would be giving rise to the same defect by providing for a republic as by providing for injustice. But that is not so. There is something absurd about the injustice provision, but not about the republic provision. There must be another explanation for the defectiveness of the article. A *moral defect* readily obtains, but this, too, is obviously still not a complete explanation. Assuming the injustice to be that certain rights are withheld from persons belonging to a certain race, then it would make no difference from the standpoint of morality if the injustice provision were stricken and replaced with a provision withholding these rights from persons of this race. It would indeed make a difference, however, from the standpoint of defectiveness; the article would no longer be absurd.

The explanation could lie in the violation of a widespread though not a necessary convention for drawing up constitutional texts, that is to say, the defect is a *conventional defect*. Without a doubt, a widespread convention is being violated, although this, too, is by itself still not a complete explanation. The rule that was violated is more than a mere convention, for it cannot be changed even in the event of changing circumstances and preferences. Rather, it is an essential element in the practice of framing a constitution, a point made clear by the redundancy, in a constitution, of an article like:

(2) *X* is a just state.

Only a *conceptual defect* remains then. I use the term 'conceptual defect' broadly here, as referring also to violations of rules that are constitutive for speech acts, that is, linguistic expressions qua actions. The claim to correctness—in this case as, above all, a claim to justice—is necessarily attached to the act of framing a constitution. A constitutional framer gives rise to a performative contradiction if the content of his act of framing a constitution negates the claim to justice, even though he makes this very claim in acting to frame a constitution.[66]

In the second example addressing the objection to the argument from correctness, a judge hands down the decision:

(1) The accused is sentenced to life imprisonment, which is wrong.

This proposition requires interpretation. The judge may want to say that his decision contradicts positive law. He may also want to say, however, that although his decision does comply with positive law, the decision is unjust. These and other interpretations lead to numerous problems that shall be set aside here. Only the following interpretation is of interest:

(2) The accused is sentenced to life imprisonment, which is an incorrect interpretation of prevailing law.

In handing down this decision, the judge without a doubt abandons his social role, and he violates rules of positive law that, surely in all legal systems, obligate him to interpret prevailing law correctly. But he would also be violating social rules if he were unshaven and wearing a filthy robe as he handed down the decision, and rules of positive law would also be violated by the decision if the interpretation were indeed incorrect, but the judge believed and claimed it to be correct. Conversely, there would still be a defect even if the judge were to assume erroneously that his interpretation is incorrect and he did not violate positive law by announcing in

---

[66] In this respect there exists a certain analogy to J. L. Austin's well-known example: '[T]he cat is on the mat but I do not believe it is.' Austin, *How to Do Things with Words*, ed. J. O. Urmson (Oxford: Clarendon Press, 1962), 48, and see at 48–50; see also Austin, 'The Meaning of a Word', in Austin, *Philosophical Papers*, 1st edn., ed. J. O. Urmson and G. J. Warnock (Oxford: Clarendon Press, 1961), 23–43, at 31–2; 2nd edn. (1970), 55–75, at 63–4.

his decision this erroneous assumption. Clearly what we have here is more than a violation of social or legal rules.[67] The judge gives rise to a performative contradiction and, in this sense, a conceptual defect. With a judicial decision, the claim is always made that the law is being correctly applied, however ill satisfied the claim may be. The very claim made in carrying out the institutional act of sentencing is contradicted by the content of the decision.

These two examples show that participants in a legal system necessarily, on all sorts of levels, lay claim to correctness. If and in so far as this claim has moral implications, a conceptually necessary connection between law and morality is demonstrated.

This still does not prove the connection thesis, of course. A positivist can endorse the argument from correctness and nevertheless insist on the separation thesis. Two strategies are available to him. First, he can show that the failure to satisfy the claim to correctness does not by itself lead to forfeiture of legal character. Apart from the limiting case of the system of norms that in no way makes the claim, the claim to correctness establishes at best a qualifying, not a classifying connection. Thus, the separation thesis, at any rate in so far as it is geared to a classifying connection, is not affected by the argument from correctness, apart from the limiting case just mentioned. A second strategy is to maintain that the claim to correctness, having a trivial content lacking in moral implications, cannot lead to a conceptually necessary connection between law and morality. The positivist's first objection points toward the argument from injustice, the second toward the argument from principles.

---

[67] Ulfrid Neumann, in *Juristische Argumentationslehre* (Darmstadt: Wissenschaftliche Buchgesellschaft, 1986), 87–8, is of a different opinion. He refers to the following example: 'In the name of the people, Mr. N. is sentenced to ten years in prison although there are no good reasons for this sentence.'

(ii) The Argument from Injustice

The argument from injustice, as noted earlier, can be applied to individual norms or to legal systems as a whole. I consider it first with reference to individual norms.

(a) Individual Norms

This version of the argument has it that legal character is forfeited when individual norms of a legal system cross a certain threshold of injustice. Its best-known variant is Radbruch's formula, which has already been discussed and rejected from the standpoint of an observer.[68] The question now is whether or not the argument from injustice, as expressed in Radbruch's formula, is acceptable from the standpoint of a participant. It should be emphasized here that Radbruch's formula does not say that a norm forfeits its legal character simply if it is unjust. The threshold is set higher than that. Legal character is forfeited only if the injustice reaches an 'intolerable degree'. Ordinance 11, pursuant to the Statute on Reich Citizenship, serves once again as our example.

There is widespread agreement today that the debate surrounding Radbruch's formula cannot be decided on the basis of analytical or conceptual arguments alone. What matters is expedient or adequate concept formation that is justified by normative arguments.[69] To be sure, the argument from correctness has a role to play in evaluating normative arguments for and against the argument from injustice. The earlier statement to the effect that the argument from correctness is the basis of the argument from injustice, too, was meant in exactly this sense.

The many and diverse positions taken in the debate surrounding Radbruch's formula can be essentially summarized

---

[68] See above, this text, at 28–31.
[69] See above, this text, at 20–3.

under eight rubrics—language, clarity, effectiveness, legal certainty, relativism, democracy, dispensability, and candour.

Language. In view of the ambiguity and vagueness of the expression 'law', a compelling linguistic-conceptual case cannot be made either for or against the argument from injustice. What can be defended, however, is the normative thesis that the inclusion of moral elements in the concept of law, required by the argument from injustice, leads to an inexpedient specification of language. So it is that Hoerster reproached the non-positivist—say, one who will not classify Ordinance 11 as law—for failing 'to say which ordinary word in our language could substitute for his morally charged concept of law, lending it a value-neutral function.'[70] The non-positivist, according to Hoerster, loses out on the possibility of generally identifying a norm like Ordinance 11 in a readily intelligible way; that can be done without difficulty only by calling it 'law'.

As noted above, this is correct from the standpoint of an observer.[71] That things change, however, if one adopts the participant's perspective can be shown with the help of the dichotomy between norm and procedure discussed earlier. The observer sees Ordinance 11 as the *result* or product of a norm-creating procedure in which other persons have participated. Similarly, a judge's decision based on Ordinance 11 is, for the observer, the result of a procedure, namely, a norm-applying procedure, in which the observer has not participated. If norm and decision agree, there is no reason for him not to call both 'law'. If the two do not agree, he faces the question of whether he should describe a contradiction or determine derogating judge-made law. A different picture emerges from the participant's perspective. To be sure, the participant—say, the judge—also sees Ordinance 11 as first of all the result of a norm-creating procedure. For him, though, this is simply the way to a second quality of Ordinance 11,

---

[70] Hoerster, *LR* 187; Hoerster, *VT* 27.
[71] See above, this text, at 30–1.

namely, that it is the *point of departure* for a norm-applying procedure in which he participates and whose result is accompanied by the claim to correctness.

Our concern here is not yet with substantive arguments, but simply with the expedient use of the expression 'law'. In order that such considerations of linguistic usage not prejudice substantive arguments, they must be compatible with different substantive theses. Take the substantive thesis that there are good legal reasons for the judge not to apply Ordinance 11 but instead to hand down a decision that contradicts its language. Given this presupposition, it would be unsatisfactory for the judge to say that Ordinance 11 is law. He must characterize his decision as 'law' since he is deciding on the basis of legal reasons. Since his decision contradicts Ordinance 11, then if he were also to classify Ordinance 11 as 'law', he would be characterizing contradictory norms as 'law', namely, the general norm established by the Ordinance and the individual norm expressed by his decision. This contradiction can be resolved without difficulty if the judge says that Ordinance 11 is indeed prima-facie law but in the end not law at all. What is expressed thereby is that, in the course of the norm-applying procedure, Ordinance 11 is denied legal character. If there are good legal reasons for not applying Ordinance 11, then not only is it possible for the judge to say that the Ordinance is in the end not law, it is necessary that he do so in order to avoid a contradiction. Thus, Hoerster's argument from language would be correct only if there could not ever be good legal reasons for deciding contrary to the language of a statute that is unjust in the extreme. If there can be such reasons in some case or another, then Hoerster's argument is incorrect from the participant's perspective. Whether there can or cannot ever be good legal reasons of this kind, however, is a substantive question not to be decided on the basis of considerations of expedient linguistic usage. This means that Hoerster's argument from language cannot justify objecting to the inclusion of moral elements in a concept of law that is seen as adequate from the participant's perspective. On the contrary, if substantive reasons speak in favour of such inclusion, linguistic usage has to fall in line.

Clarity. The second argument in the debate surrounding Radbruch's formula is made in terms of clarity. H. L. A. Hart offers a classic formulation:

[I]f we adopt Radbruch's view, and with him and the German courts make our protest against evil law in the form of an assertion that certain rules cannot be law because of their moral iniquity, we confuse one of the most powerful, because it is the simplest, forms of moral criticism. If with the Utilitarians we speak plainly, we say that laws may be law but too evil to be obeyed. This is a moral condemnation which everyone can understand and it makes an immediate and obvious claim to moral attention. If, on the other hand, we formulate our objection as an assertion that these evil things are not law, here is an assertion which many people do not believe, and if they are disposed to consider it at all, it would seem to raise a whole host of philosophical issues before it can be accepted . . . [W]hen we have the ample resources of plain speech we must not present the moral criticism of institutions as propositions of a disputable philosophy.[72]

On first glance, this objection cannot be denied a certain legitimacy. A positivistic concept of law that renounces the inclusion of any moral elements at all is simpler and at least in this respect clearer than a concept of law that includes moral elements. Another consideration, however, is that clarity in terms of simplicity is not the only goal of concept formation. Simplicity must not prevail at the expense of adequacy.[73] Moreover, even a complex concept can be clear. One scarcely need fear that jurists will be confused by the inclusion of moral elements in the concept of law.[74] Jurists are accustomed to dealing with complicated concepts. For the citizen, what

[72] Hart, *PSLM* 620–1, repr. Hart, *Essays* 77–8. Similarly Hoerster, *LR* 187–8; Hoerster, *VR* 2481–2.

[73] See Walter Ott, 'Die Radbruch'sche Formel. Pro und Contra', *Zeitschrift für Schweizerisches Recht*, N.F. (new series) 107 (1988), 335–57, at 343.

[74] ibid. 349–50.

gives rise to a lack of clarity is not primarily that moral elements are included in the concept of law. He might also be confused by the news that even extreme injustice is law. Rather, what gives rise to a lack of clarity is that it is not easy, in many cases, to draw the line between norms that are unjust in the extreme and norms that are not. That is a problem to be addressed in terms of legal certainty, however, not clarity. The objection based on clarity is concerned only with whether or not moral elements are to be included at all in the concept of law.

A general kind of conceptual indeterminacy, then, is not the focus of the argument adduced in terms of clarity by Hart and Hoerster. Rather, the question is how a conflict between law and morality is to be comprehended conceptually. Neither Hart nor Hoerster would resolve the conflict even in the case of extreme injustice. What the law demands is one thing, what morality requires is another. That is, morality can permit or require the jurist, as human being and citizen, to refuse to obey the law, but what he refuses to obey is still the law. Every other account serves 'to cloak the true nature of the problems with which we are faced'.[75] The positivist can discuss the questions associated with statutory injustice 'unveiled as what they are, namely, questions of ethics'. The non-positivist, by contrast, runs the 'risk of hiding their ethical character by shifting them, by definition, into the concept of law'.[76]

Is this objection justified? Is the problem being cloaked, veiled, and hidden by the non-positivist? The answer is no. The non-positivist does not deny the ethical character of the problem. He simply claims that, in the case of extreme injustice, the ethical problem is also a legal problem. The result is that he draws legal conclusions from his moral judgment. The content of his argumentation may coincide with that of the positivist's, and he, too, must lay out his arguments and open them up for discussion. That he moves, in the case of extreme

---

[75] Hart, *PSLM* 620, repr. Hart, *Essays* 77.
[76] Hoerster, *LR* 187.

injustice, away from the standpoint of morality to the stand-point of the law is not a veiling of the problem, but, rather, the expression of a substantive thesis. And this thesis can be attacked only with substantive arguments, not with a formal argument charging a lack of clarity. The remaining objection is to a 'disputable philosophy' that 'would seem to raise a whole host of philosophical issues'[77] and could therefore lead to a lack of clarity and to confusion. But this objection can be held against positivism, too, which also gives expression to a certain legal philosophy that can be debated. In this debate, positivism and non-positivism are, in principle, on equal footing in direct opposition to one another. That positivism cannot pretend to anything like a presumption of correctness is shown by the claim to correctness that is necessarily attached to the law, a claim that speaks more in favour of non-positivism. Thus, the non-positivist cannot be dislodged by an argument adduced in terms of clarity either.

Effectiveness.   Before the era of National Socialism in Ger-many,[78] Radbruch was a legal positivist—not in terms of justi-fication, to be sure,[79] but in terms of result, at any rate where the judge is concerned.[80] After 1945, Radbruch changed his mind and defended the view that legal positivism 'rendered both jurist and the people defenceless against arbitrary, cruel, criminal statutes, however extreme'.[81] He now demanded the inclusion of moral elements in the concept of law in order to 'arm jurists against the recurrence of a rogue state (*Unrechts-staat*)' like Nazi Germany.[82] Hart objected that it was naïve to assume that a non-positivistic definition of the law could have

---

[77] Hart, *PSLM* 621, 620, repr. Hart, *Essays* 78.
[78] (This sentence of the original text has been modified by the author.)
[79] See Arthur Kaufmann, *Rechtsphilosophie*, 2nd edn. (Munich: C. H. Beck, 1997), at 41–4.
[80] See Radbruch, *LP* § 10 (at pp. 116–20).
[81] Gustav Radbruch, 'Five Minutes of Legal Philosophy', trans. Stanley L. Paulson, in *Philosophy of Law*, 3rd edn., ed. Joel Feinberg and Hyman Gross (Belmont, Calif.: Wadsworth, 1986), 109–10, at 109 (trans. altered).
[82] Radbruch, *GUR* 107, *RGA 3* 90.

any effect on statutory lawlessness.[83] Hart's argument, directed to the effectiveness of the non-positivistic concept of law, was fine-tuned by Hoerster. According to him, the expectations that Radbruch attaches to this concept are based on an 'enormous overestimation'[84] of the effect the legal theorist or philosopher has on the behaviour of citizens and jurists.

For one cannot change reality simply through the definition of a concept. A statute that is morally dubious but enacted within the framework of the prevailing legal system—whether the legal philosopher calls it 'valid law' or not—possesses, apart from its immorality, all the qualities that a morally impeccable statute possesses: It has come into being in accordance with the prevailing constitution. It is applied and enforced by a legal staff. And whoever refuses to obey it (say, because of its immorality) must reckon with the usual consequences of a violation of law. One cannot dispose of all these facts by deciding in favour of the anti-positivistic, morally charged definition of the concept of law.[85]

The thesis that a non-positivistic concept of law has no effect on statutory lawlessness can be sharpened into the claim that such a concept is not only not helpful, it is in fact a hindrance in the struggle against statutory lawlessness. Positivism, with its strict separation of legal and moral obligations, encourages a critical stance vis-à-vis the law. By contrast, one who begins by including moral elements in the concept of law runs the risk of uncritically identifying legal with moral requirements. So it is that Kelsen rejects the thesis 'that only a moral social system is law', offering as his reason: '... such a system, in its actual application by the jurisprudence prevailing in a particular legal community, leads to an uncritical legitimation of the state coercive system constituting this community.'[86] Within the framework of the argument

---

[83] Cf. Hart, *PSLM* 617–18, repr. Hart, *Essays* 74; Hart, *CL* 205, 2nd edn. 209–10.

[84] Hoerster, *LR* 185.

[85] ibid. 186.

[86] Kelsen, *PTL* § 13 (pp. 68–9) (trans. altered); in agreement, Hoerster, *VT* 32; see also Horst Dreier, 'Die Radbruchsche Formel—Erkenntnis oder

adduced in terms of effectiveness, there are, then, two theses to be distinguished. The first says that a non-positivistic concept of law can have no effect on statutory lawlessness. The second has it that a non-positivistic concept of law carries with it the risk of uncritically legitimating statutory lawlessness. The latter thesis goes further, and I shall consider it first.

The risk of uncritical legitimation would indeed exist if the non-positivistic connection thesis said that a norm is a legal norm only if its content corresponds to morality. It is this variant of the connection thesis that Kelsen and Hoerster have in mind when they formulate their objection in terms of uncritical legitimation. Thus, Kelsen speaks of the 'thesis that the law is in its essence moral'.[87] According to Hoerster, the connection thesis runs: 'A norm is legal only if it is moral', which is logically equivalent to 'if a norm is legal, it is moral'.[88] If the point of departure is this version of the connection thesis, which may be called the 'strong' version, then every jurist who characterizes a norm as a legal norm must at the same time classify it as morally justified. That would indeed carry with it the risk of an uncritical legitimation of the law.

The objection in terms of uncritical legitimation fails to recognize, however, that a non-positivist need not defend the strong connection thesis, with its postulate of a contentual agreement between every legal norm and morality. Radbruch's formula says expressly, 'The positive law, secured by legislation and power, takes precedence even when its content is unjust and inexpedient'.[89] Legal character, according to the formula, is forfeited only if the conflict between law and morality reaches an 'intolerable', that is, an extreme degree. This may be called the 'weak' connection thesis.

The weak connection thesis does not lead to an identification of the law with morality. It says that unjust and therefore

Bekenntnis?' in *Staatsrecht in Theorie und Praxis. Festschrift Robert Walter zum 60. Geburtstag*, ed. Heinz Mayer *et al.* (Vienna: Manz, 1991), 133.

[87] Kelsen, *PTL* § 13 (p. 68) (trans. altered).
[88] Hoerster, *VT* 32.
[89] Radbruch, *GUR* 107, *RGA* 3 89.

immoral norms can be law. So, like legal positivism, it admits of a moral critique of the law and, in this respect, makes possible a critical stance vis-à-vis the law. It differs from legal positivism simply in that beyond a certain threshold, legal character is forfeited. Now, one might think that this alone suffices for uncritical legitimation. Jurists would be inclined to say that the threshold has not been crossed, therefore their legal system possesses at least a minimum moral legitimacy. A counter-argument, however, lies in the character of the threshold. The threshold is extreme injustice. The formulation found in the Federal Constitutional Court decision on citizenship, referred to above, serves as an example. 'The attempt to destroy physic-ally and materially, in accordance with "racist" criteria, certain parts of one's own population, including women and children, has nothing in common with law and justice.'[90]

If any moral judgments can be justified in terms of the claim to universal bindingness,[91] then surely it is those that charac-terize as immoral and unjust in the extreme the pursuit of goals like this. The threshold beyond which norms forfeit legal character is marked by minimum moral requirements. An example is the elementary human right to life and physical security. The claim is made that moral requirements like this, at any rate, can be rationally justified.[92] If this is so, then one scarcely need fear something like an 'uncritical legitimation' of norms that are beyond the threshold of extreme injustice. Such legitimation would at least cause some trouble—which may be one reason that barbaric acts of injustice are often carried out not in accordance with proper legal form but on the strength of more or less secret orders.[93]

---

[90] *BVerfGE* 23 (1968), 98, at 106.

[91] (This sentence of the original text has been modified by the author.)

[92] See Robert Alexy, 'A Discourse-Theoretical Conception of Practical Reason', trans. Ruth Adler and Neil MacCormick, *Ratio Juris*, 5 (1992), 231–51.

[93] See on this issue Walter Ott, 'Der Euthanasie-Befehl Hitlers vom 1. September 1939 im Lichte der rechtspositivistischen Theorien', in *Staats-recht in Theorie und Praxis* (n. 86 above), 519–33.

There is, then, a double conclusion to report. Below the threshold of extreme injustice, the weak connection thesis—as expressed, say, in Radbruch's formula—does not run the risk of uncritical legitimation, because a conflict between law and morality at this level does not rule out legal character. And beyond the threshold of extreme injustice, there is at any rate no risk of uncritical legitimation if the minimum moral requirements that mark the threshold can be rationally justified. In passing, I might point out that an uncritical legitimation of currently prevailing law is also possible from the positivistic standpoint of strict separation of law and morality, for contentual agreement can be claimed even on the basis of conceptual separation.

Within the framework of the argument adduced in terms of effectiveness, the other objection to the non-positivistic concept of law has it that such a concept can have no effect on statutory lawlessness. This objection charging ineffectiveness is to a considerable extent legitimate. Hart and Hoerster are correct in saying that definitions of the concept of law that are offered by legal theory or legal philosophy cannot, as such, change reality. It makes no essential difference to a judge in a rogue state whether, in refusing to apply a statute that is unjust in the extreme, he appeals to Hart and refuses on *moral* grounds or joins Radbruch and refuses on *legal* grounds.[94] Either way, he has to reckon with personal consequences, and his willingness to make this sacrifice turns on factors other than the definition of the concept of law.

Still, there are differences from the standpoint of effectiveness. One difference is clear if the focus is on legal practice rather than on the individual judge, who measures statutory lawlessness or injustice against his conscience.[95] If there exists in legal practice a consensus that the satisfaction of certain minimum requirements of justice is a necessary

---

[94] See Ott, 'Die Radbruch'sche Formel. Pro und Contra' (n. 73 above), at 346.

[95] ibid. 347.

presupposition for the legal character of state directives, then not only is there a line of moral argumentation available for resisting the acts of a rogue regime, there is also, anchored in legal practice, a line of legal argumentation. One ought to have no illusions, though, about the prospects for the success of such resistance. A rogue regime that is halfway successful can quickly destroy the legal practitioners' consensus by intimidating individuals, making personnel changes, and rewarding conformity. It is at least conceivable, however, that this fails to work for a weaker rogue regime, especially in its initial phase. Granted, this is a relatively limited effect, but it is an effect. What is important is that even if this relatively limited effect should prove to be an erroneous assumption, no compelling objection to the non-positivistic concept of law results. To defend his position, the non-positivist does not need to show that, in a rogue state, his concept of law makes a better safeguard against statutory lawlessness than the positivistic concept of law does. It is enough that the struggle against statutory lawlessness can be just as effectively waged on the basis of the non-positivistic concept of law as on the basis of a positivistic concept of law. And that much is certain. For why should it not be the case that the struggle can be just as effectively waged when statutory lawlessness or injustice is not seen as law as when it is seen as law?

Once a rogue state is successfully established, legal concepts may no longer have much effect. Only after the collapse of such a state are essential differences between the positivist and the non-positivist evident. Still, even in the successfully established rogue state, the non-positivistic concept of law does have one slight but not unimportant effect that can work against statutory lawlessness. It may be called the 'risk effect'. A judge or another office-holder in a rogue state sees his own situation differently according to whether he interprets it in light of a positivistic or a non-positivistic concept of law. A judge, for example, faces the question of whether or not he should hand down a terroristic criminal sentence that is covered by lawless or unjust statutes. He is neither a saint nor a hero. He has little interest in the fate of the accused, but more interest in his own. All historical experience says that he cannot rule out the collapse of the rogue state, and he worries about what might happen to him then. If he has to assume the predominant or general acceptance of a non-positivistic concept of law according to which the norm supporting the terroristic sentence is not law, then he takes a relatively high risk of being unable to justify himself later and therefore of being prosecuted. The risk diminishes if he can be certain that his behaviour will be evaluated later on the basis of a positivistic concept of law. To be sure, the risk does not disappear altogether, for a retroactive statute may be enacted that could hold him accountable. Still, the risk is a lesser one. Retroactive statutes pose problems for the *Rechtsstaat* or rule of law, so it is entirely possible that no such statute will be enacted, and if one is, our judge can nevertheless try to defend himself by claiming to have acted on the basis of formerly valid law. It is clear, then, that a predominant or general acceptance of a non-positivistic concept of law increases the risk of those persons who, in a rogue state, commit or participate in committing lawless or unjust acts that are covered by statute. Thus, even for persons who see no real reason not to be involved in injustice, or who would actually favour such involvement, an incentive arises or is reinforced for them not to participate in injustice at all or at least to tone it down. In this way, the predominant or general acceptance of a non-positivistic concept of law can have an affirmative effect even in a rogue state. All in all, therefore, one can say that the practical consequences of the non-positivistic concept of law, from the point of view of fighting statutory lawlessness, are at any rate not worse and in some respects even better than those of the positivistic concept of law.

Legal Certainty. A fourth argument against the non-positivistic concept of law asserts that this concept jeopardizes legal certainty. The argument does indeed count against variants of non-positivism that take as their point of departure a strong connection thesis, that is, those variants according to which every injustice leads to the forfeiture of legal character. If, in addition, every person is given the authority, appealing to his own notion of justice, to refuse to comply with statutes, then the argument from jeopardized legal certainty is magnified into the argument from anarchy. This need not be pursued further, however, for no serious non-positivist defends such views. Here, the question is simply whether or not legal certainty is jeopardized by a concept of law that entails the forfeiture of legal character not in every case of injustice, but only in cases of extreme injustice. The answer to the question is no.

If there are notions of justice that are rationally justifiable, then one who rationally justifies his view that an action is unjust can be said to know this. Now, the following principle applies: the more extreme the injustice, the more certain the knowledge of it. This principle connects material and epistemological considerations. It provides a justification for the Federal Constitutional Court's view, stated in the decision on citizenship discussed above, not only that the injustice of Ordinance 11 reached an 'intolerable degree', but also that this was 'evident'.[96] There may well be cases, of course, in which one cannot say with complete certainty whether or not extreme injustice is at hand. This scarcely counts at all, however, when compared with the uncertainties generally attending knowledge of the law. The non-positivistic connection thesis leads at most, then, to a minimal loss of legal certainty.

An answer to the question of whether this minimal loss of legal certainty is acceptable must take into account that while legal certainty is indeed an important value, it is not the only value. The value of legal certainty must be weighed against the value of material justice.[97] Radbruch's formula makes an assessment that fundamentally gives precedence to

---

[96] *BVerfGE* 23 (1968), 98, at 106.
[97] Radbruch, *GUR* 107, *RGA 3* 88–9.

legal certainty and only in extreme cases inverts the relation. The only one who can object to this at all is one who regards legal certainty as an absolute principle.[98] And that, like every pursuit of an absolute principle, has an air of fanaticism about it.

Relativism. The argument adduced in terms of legal certainty is sharpened by the argument from relativism. It says that not only is it difficult to recognize the boundary between injustice that is and is not extreme, but no notion of justice, not even of extreme injustice, can be rationally justified or objectively known. This is the thesis of radical relativism. If this thesis is correct, then the inclusion of moral elements in the concept of law means nothing other than that the judge, in cases where his subjective preferences are especially intensely affected, is offered the possibility of deciding contrary to the statute. Hoerster paints a drastic picture:

There is no guarantee, not even the mere likelihood, that the morality the judge or the citizen in question brings into his concept of law is in fact an 'enlightened' morality... Nothing says in general that the moral notions of some particular individual or of some particular society are in some sense or another more enlightened (say, 'more humane' or 'more just') than the positive legal norms of the state in question... It is not exactly as if there were only—as the opponents of legal positivism are always suggesting—the judge or the citizen who, confronted with 'Nazi statutes', would rather pay heed to a humane morality. There is just as well the judge or the citizen who, confronted with 'democratic' statutes (say, those of the Weimar Republic or of the post-war Bonn Republic), would rather pay heed to a Nazi morality.[99]

The argument from relativism makes explicit what was already obvious as a presupposition in the arguments adduced in terms of effectiveness and legal certainty: The non-positivist presupposes an at least rudimentary non-relativistic ethics. It is no accident that Radbruch, before 1933, establishes

[98] On the concept of an absolute principle, see Alexy, *TCR*, at 62–4.
[99] Hoerster, *VR* 2482.

his in effect positivistic view[100] by appealing to relativism, that is, by appealing to the thesis that a universally compelling justification of moral principles is impossible.

Now, however, it has proved to be impossible to answer the question as to the purpose of the law other than by listing the diverse opinions of interested parties. And it is precisely on this alone, on this impossibility of a natural law, that the validity of the positive law can be established; at this point, relativism—simply our method of observation until now—is itself admitted as a building block into our system.[101]

After 1945, Radbruch extracts a basic repertory of human and civil rights from relativistic scepticism:

Certainly [these legal principles, called natural law or the law of reason,] are surrounded by doubt when it comes to particulars, but the work of centuries has nevertheless developed a solid repertory, collected with such broad consensus in the so-called declarations of human and civil rights that, with respect to some of them, only a labored scepticism can still harbour doubts.[102]

The references to historical experience—'the work of centuries'—and to an actually existent 'broad' consensus still do not amount to a refutation of relativism, even if in terms of national, supranational, and international legal practice these factual references approach such a refutation. A sceptic may object that the development of moral views over the last centuries or millennia has gone off the track, and that it is possible that everyone or nearly everyone is entangled in a collective mistake. To dispel this sceptical objection, one must show that one can rationally justify a proposition like:

(1) The physical and material destruction of a minority of the population on grounds of race is injustice in the extreme.

---

[100] (This sentence of the original text has been modified by the author.)
[101] Radbruch, *LP* § 10 (p. 116) (trans. altered).
[102] Radbruch, 'Five Minutes of Legal Philosophy' (n. 81 above), 110 (trans. altered).

Showing this is *eo ipso* to show that one can rationally refute a proposition like:

(2) The physical and material destruction of a minority of the population on grounds of race is not injustice in the extreme.

The problem of legal positivism leads, then, to the meta-ethical problem of the justifiability of moral judgments. I shall not discuss this problem here,[103] resting content with the claim that a proposition like (1) is rationally justifiable and a proposition like (2) is rationally refutable. If this claim is correct, then the objection based on relativism is answered. If this claim is not correct, then to counter the objection based on relativism, one could only—but could at least—point to the fact of a currently broad consensus, which is not in itself, to be sure, a refutation in the strict sense but which does, for legal practice, as mentioned above, approach a refutation.

What this means with respect to Hoerster's concern that a judge faced with democratically enacted, just statutes could appeal to a 'Nazi morality' is that such a judge, at any rate in a state steeped in the tradition of human rights or open to them, should be thwarted by the fact of a broad consensus on fundamental rights. Furthermore, if rationally justified notions of extreme injustice are possible, then there are rational grounds for not resisting democratically enacted statutes by appealing to a 'Nazi morality'. Only in a society already given over in its majority to a 'Nazi morality' does a serious risk exist that a judge, appealing to a non-positivistic concept of law, will deny legal character to just statutes because he finds intolerable a violation of 'Nazi morality'. That the non-positivistic concept of law may be misused this way in such a society is a drawback, but not one that is all that weighty. Once 'Nazi morality' achieves dominance, statutes conflicting with it to an extreme degree do not last long anyway.

---

[103] See Alexy, *TLA*, at 33–100; Alexy, 'On Necessary Relations between Law and Morality' (n. 43 above).

Democracy. What has been said here about the objection based on relativism can be applied to another possible objection to the non-positivistic concept of law, the objection based on democracy. It says that the non-positivistic concept of law carries with it the risk that the judge, appealing to justice, will oppose decisions of the democratically legitimated legislator.[104] Since this would amount to an intrusion of the judiciary into the sphere of the legislature, the objection can also be formulated in terms of jeopardizing the separation of powers.

This objection loses its punch if one considers that the non-positivistic concept of law entails the forfeiture of legal character only in cases of extreme injustice. It has an effect only in a core area. The content of the constitutional review of rights violations in democratic constitutional states reaches much further. Whoever appeals to democracy or the separation of powers to argue against the weak connection thesis represented here would have to reject any judicial review whatsoever of the legislator's commitment to fundamental rights.

Dispensability.   Radbruch's formula is of practical significance above all after the collapse of a rogue regime. The Federal Constitutional Court's decision on citizenship discussed above serves as an example of this. By contrast, the objection based on dispensability says that statutory injustice can be accounted for other than by revoking legal character. That is, the new legislator can abrogate the unjust older statute by means of a retroactive statute.[105]

In order to assess correctly the objection based on dispensability, criminal cases must be distinguished from other cases. Art. 103, para. 2, of the Basic Law[106] formulates an elementary principle of the *Rechtsstaat*, namely, *nulla poena sine*

---

[104] Ingeborg Maus, 'Die Trennung von Recht und Moral als Begrenzung des Rechts', *Rechtstheorie*, 20 (1989), 191–210, at 193: 'The moral argument can...easily be misused as a substitute for democracy.'

[105] Hart, *PSLM* 619, repr. Hart, *Essays* 77.

[106] *GG* art. 103, para. 2: 'An act may be punished only if it was defined by a law as a criminal offense before the act was committed' (trans. altered).

lege,[107] as a norm of positive constitutional law, thereby proscribing the enactment of retroactive criminal statutes by the ordinary legislator. This can be generalized. If the principle *nulla poena sine lege* has constitutional status, then one can hardly say in the field of criminal law that the enactment of a retroactive ordinary statute would render dispensable the application of a non-positivistic concept of law. Certainly one could imagine a constitutional change that, in cases of extreme injustice, would permit exceptions to the principle *nulla poena sine lege*—and thereby exceptions to the principle *nullum crimen sine lege*,[108] too. Such exceptions would be problematic at the least, however, under a constitution that—as the Basic Law does in art. 79, para. 3[109]—withholds the competence to change elementary principles of the *Rechtsstaat* even from the legislator empowered to change the constitution. Accompanying this legal problem is a factual one. Even if it should be legally permissible to attach an exceptions-clause to the principle *nulla poena sine lege*, it would be highly doubtful that such a clause could garner the qualified majority necessary for changing the constitution. All of this shows that merely referring to the legislator does not establish in all legal systems and under all circumstances the dispensability of Radbruch's formula.

If the principle *nulla poena sine lege* has constitutional status and is unchangeable, or if it does not formally have constitutional status but, as a fundamental legal principle, cannot be restricted, then the real problem in criminal law cases is not that a non-positivistic concept of law is dispensable, but, rather, whether or not the application of such a concept of law leads to a *circumvention* of the principle *nulla poena sine lege*. To be sure, this problem is not identical with

---

[107] 'Without a law, there is no punishment.'
[108] 'Without a law, there is no crime.'
[109] *GG* art. 79, para. 3: 'Amendments of this Basic Law affecting the division of the Federation into *Länder*, the participation in principle of the *Länder* in legislation, or the basic principles laid down in articles 1 and 20 shall be inadmissible.'

the problem of dispensability, and I take it up within the framework of the next objection, based on candour.

In essence, then, the appeal to dispensability is restricted to cases outside the field of criminal law, cases where there exists in principle the possibility of solving the problem of lawless or unjust statutes by means of retroactive statutes. The question, though, is what the judge ought to do if the legislator, for whatever reason, fails to act and if the lawless or unjust statute cannot, on the basis of currently prevailing constitutional law, be declared irrelevant for the decision at hand. Should the judge, then, hand down decisions based on, and themselves representing, injustice in the extreme? One might think that the judge should go ahead and do this in order to prompt the legislator to enact retroactive statutes. But that would mean in numerous cases, especially in the civil law, that the affected citizen suffers a disadvantageous decision based on, and itself representing, injustice in the extreme, simply to prompt the legislator to react. Thus, the citizen would be used, permanently or temporarily, as a means of provoking legislative activity. That cannot be reconciled with his fundamental rights, which shows that pointing out the mere possibility of a retroactive statute is not enough to demonstrate that the application of a non-positivistic concept of law is dispensable. If the legislator fails to make use of this possibility, and if the lawless or unjust statute cannot, on the basis of currently prevailing constitutional law, be declared irrelevant for the decision at hand, then a non-positivistic concept of law must of necessity be applied in order to protect the fundamental rights of the citizen.

Along with this counter-argument, focused on the rights of the citizen, comes a second, based on the claim to correctness. As discussed above, every judicial decision necessarily lays claim to correctness. A decision based on, and itself representing, injustice in the extreme fails in the extreme to satisfy this claim. So there are, outside the field of criminal law, two grounds for refuting the argument from dispensability and maintaining that a non-positivistic concept of law is indispensable: respect for the rights of the citizen and the claim to correctness.

Candour. The objection based on candour says that, in criminal law cases, the non-positivistic concept of law leads to a circumvention of the principle *nulla poena sine lege*. Hart illustrates this argument with a case decided in 1949 by a German court of appeals.[110] A woman who wanted to be rid of her husband told the authorities in 1944 that he had made disparaging comments about Hitler while home on leave from the front. The husband was arrested and, pursuant to provisions imposing criminal liability for such remarks, sentenced to death. He was not executed, but sent to the front instead. In 1949, the wife was prosecuted for depriving her husband of his liberty. The Court of Appeals in Bamberg, which finally heard the case, found her guilty. The Court was of the opinion that the husband's death sentence was legal, since the National Socialist criminal statutes on which it was based simply prescribed 'an omission, namely, to remain silent', and for that reason it was not based on 'a statute obviously contrary to natural law'.[111] The Court condemned the wife, however, on the basis of a controversial criminal law construction according to which a deprivation of liberty perpetrated indirectly can be criminally punishable even if the direct perpetrator—here, the National Socialist court—acts legally. The Court in Bamberg held that the wife's denunciation of her husband was illegal because it 'violated the sound conscience and sense of justice of all decent human beings'. The correctness of this criminal law construction need not be discussed here.[112] Nor is it of any concern that Hart, as he himself later

---

[110] *OLG Bamberg*, reported in *Süddeutsche Juristen-Zeitung*, 5 (1950), 207–9.

[111] ibid. 208–9 (court opinion).

[112] One might enquire in particular into the implications of the thesis that the denunciation 'violated the sound conscience and sense of justice of all decent human beings' to such a degree that it was illegal and therefore punishable. Does this not imply that the death sentence resulting from the denunciation was unjust? Can the denunciation violate 'the sound

remarks,[113] represents the case incorrectly in that he supposes that the Court in Bamberg reached its conclusion by denying legal validity to the National Socialist statutes underlying the death sentence.[114] If one agrees with the Court in Bamberg that a statute permitting the death penalty for disparaging comments about a dictator does not amount to extreme injustice because it simply prescribes an omission, then one need only consider the hypothetical case of a woman who denounces her husband because, in a dictatorship, he disobeys a command, based on a statute, to commit homicidal acts of extreme injustice. Following the opinion of the Court in Bamberg, the wife would be subject to condemnation in this case because the sentence resulting from her denunciation would be illegal.

Hart objects:

There were, of course, two other choices. One was to let the woman go unpunished; one can sympathize with and endorse the view that this might have been a bad thing to do. The other was to face the fact that if the woman were to be punished it must be pursuant to the introduction of a frankly retrospective law and with a full consciousness of what was sacrificed in securing her punishment in this way. Odious as retrospective criminal legislation and punishment may be, to have pursued it openly in this case would at least have had the merits of candour. It would have made plain that in punishing the woman a choice had to be made between two evils, that of leaving her unpunished and that of sacrificing a very precious principle of morality endorsed by most legal systems.[115]

The objection based on candour is the strongest argument against the non-positivistic concept of law, but not its down-

conscience and sense of justice of all decent human beings' enough to be illegal and therefore punishable, even if the death sentence was in no way unjust? If one answers 'no' to the latter question, then the decisive question is whether the punishability of the denunciation simply presupposes that the death sentence was to some degree unjust, or whether it requires an extreme and therefore evident injustice of the sentence.

[113] Hart, *CL* 254–5, 2nd edn. 303–4.
[114] Hart, *PSLM* 619, repr. Hart, *Essays* 76–7.
[115] ibid.

fall. First of all, the non-positivist has a way out of Hart's dilemma. He can deny the legal character of an unjust statute that implies the right to denounce someone and can none the less arrive at exemption from criminal liability. To do this, he needs simply to apply, on specifically criminal law grounds, the principle *nulla poena sine lege* to all statutory and efficacious norms and only to these, however unjust they may be. For the field of criminal law, then, Radbruch's formula is, in order to protect the citizen, restricted by the principle *nulla poena sine lege*. Accordingly, it has an effect now only outside the criminal law. Still, another rejoinder to the appeal to candour is preferable. Radbruch's formula leads to the criminal punishment of those deeds alone whose injustice is so extreme and therefore so evident that it is more easily recognizable than the injustice in many run-of-the-mill criminal law cases.[116] That is at any rate acceptable when—as in the case of denunciation—it is not that norms establishing criminal liability are produced with the help of a non-positivistic concept of law, but, rather, that statutory injustice leading to an exclusion of criminal liability is defeated. If the injustice of these norms is so extreme and therefore so evident that everyone can clearly recognize it, then there can be no question of a covert retroactivity. For then the injustice was clearly recognizable when the deed was committed, and, because at that point it was so extreme and therefore so evident that everyone could clearly recognize it, these norms were not, at the time of the deed, law that could lead to the exclusion of criminal liability. Thus, the legal situation is not changed retroactively, but, rather, what the legal situation was at the time of the deed is simply determined. If the argument from injustice is limited to the weak connection thesis, that is, comes into play only in the event of extreme and therefore evident injustice, then there cannot be any question of a covert retroactivity and therefore not of a lack of candour either.

---

[116] As Walter Ott correctly notes in 'Die Radbruch'sche Formel. Pro und Contra' (n. 73 above), at 355.

The Results of the Enquiry into the Debate surrounding Radbruch's Formula. Applied to individual norms, the argument from injustice—in the weaker version expressed in Radbruch's formula—fares better in our enquiry than do the objections raised against it. All the objections were answered at least well enough to tie the score. And what is more, reasons were given for preferring the argument from injustice. Within the framework of one objection, the argument adduced in terms of effectiveness, a risk effect was introduced that can work to a certain extent against statutory lawlessness even in a rogue state. The necessity of applying the non-positivistic concept of law, as explained in discussing the objection based on dispensability, takes on special significance after the collapse of a rogue state. If the new legislator fails to act, and if the lawless or unjust older statute cannot, on the basis of currently prevailing constitutional law, be declared irrelevant for the decision at hand, then the necessity of applying the non-positivistic concept of law follows from respect for the rights of the citizen and from the claim to correctness necessarily made by judicial decisions. For the field of criminal law, the argument from injustice can be shown, in its weaker version, to be reconcilable with the principle *nulla poena sine lege*. It has also become clear, though, that the refutation of a number of objections depends on the possibility of a rational justification for at least some minimum moral requirements, a core repertory of elementary human rights. Should such justification prove unsuccessful, then only relative to a legal practice steeped in the tradition of human rights would the positivistic opponents of the argument from injustice be refuted. To be sure, that would not be a refutation in the strict sense, but, from a practical standpoint, it would come close.

(b) Legal Systems

The question arises of whether the argument from injustice can be applied not only to individual norms but also to legal systems as a whole. As noted above, a system of norms that neither explicitly nor implicitly lays claim to correctness is not, even from the observer's perspective, to be classified as a legal system.[117] It was also noted that this has few practical consequences, for actually existing systems of norms regularly lay claim to correctness, however feebly justified the claim may be. Practically speaking, significant problems first turn up where this claim is indeed made but not satisfied. The argument from injustice comes into play when the failure to satisfy the claim to correctness crosses the threshold of extreme injustice. Then the question is whether there are consequences that affect the legal system as a whole, that is, consequences beyond a mere summing up of the consequences of individual norms that are unjust in the extreme.

An argument like this, applied to the system as a whole, is adduced by Martin Kriele. His point of departure is the thesis that it is 'a moral obligation to comply with the law, if the law "by and large" takes morality into account'.[118] According to Kriele, this condition is satisfied when the legal system rests on the principles of the democratic constitutional state. It is not satisfied in totalitarian dictatorships. Kriele's entire argument focuses on legal obligation as moral obligation and on the related question of the legitimacy of legal systems and individual legal norms.

The question of legitimacy that Kriele asks is not the same as our question here. A lack of legitimacy need not entail a lack of legal character, and a norm classified as a legal norm may well prescribe something that is in conflict with a moral obligation. So it is that Kriele himself speaks of 'immoral law'.[119] In order to reach to the question posed here, Kriele's argument has to be reworked into an argument that focuses on legal character. The variant to be considered runs, then, as follows: A system of norms forfeits its legal character if it is by

---

[117] See above, this text, at 34.
[118] Martin Kriele, *Recht und praktische Vernunft* (Göttingen: Vandenhoeck & Ruprecht, 1979), 117.
[119] ibid. 125.

and large unjust in the extreme. This formula lends itself to different interpretations, two of which are of interest here: the extension thesis and the collapse thesis.

The Extension Thesis. The extension thesis says that a lack of legal character on the part of the fundamental substantive norms of a legal system entails a lack of legal character on the part of all norms typical of the system, and in this sense extends to them. Within the framework of his own enquiry, Kriele defends the extension thesis. This is apparent in his thesis

> that, even in a totalitarian state, there is direct statutory legitimacy, namely, the legitimacy of those statutes that are not typical of the system and, exceptionally, coincide with morality. Statutes about contract compliance, entering into marriage, the proscription of murder, as well as traffic regulations, all these are recognized as legitimate in the totalitarian state, too, because they would be justified even if measured against enlightened standards. The legitimacy of such statutes exists, then, not because of their origins in the totalitarian system—to which they are related only externally and not internally—but, rather, in spite of those origins.[120]

According to an argument structured like this, an individual norm in a legal system of extreme injustice does not forfeit its legal character only if it is itself unjust in the extreme. Legal character may be forfeited simply because a norm 'typical of the system' shares in the lawless character of the whole system, even though the norm itself may not cross the threshold of extreme injustice. Thus, the extension thesis leads to a typical case of an argument from the whole to its parts. A single element, because it is part of a whole that has a particular property, is supposed to have this particular property, which it would not have if considered in isolation. Such an argument from the whole to its parts can indeed easily explain how it is that, in the case of extreme injustice, the legal

---

[120] Martin Kriele, *Recht und praktische Vernunft* (Göttingen: Vandenhoeck & Ruprecht, 1979), 125–6.

character of a system of norms as a whole has consequences that go beyond a mere summing up of the consequences of individual norms that are unjust in the extreme. The question is whether the extension thesis and thereby the argument from the whole to its parts is acceptable. The decisive point in answering this question is that what is at issue is not moral correctness, justice, or the preservation of enlightened standards but, rather, legal character. In discussing the argument from injustice applied to individual norms, as expressed in Radbruch's formula, legal certainty is shown to be a central argument against denying the legal character of norms that are authoritatively issued and socially efficacious; only in cases of extreme injustice, because they are relatively easy to recognize, was it possible to rebuff the argument adduced in terms of legal certainty. The same applies to legal systems as a whole. Legal certainty would be too severely compromised if a norm below the threshold of extreme injustice were to forfeit its legal character because it somehow shares in the injustice of the whole system and is therefore typical of it. A norm can share to a greater or lesser degree in the injustice of the whole system. A norm can be to a greater or lesser degree typical of the system. Should its legal character be revoked by any degree of participation whatsoever, even a modest one? If so, how is a norm to be recognized as sharing in the injustice of the whole system, even if only modestly? Is that already the case when a norm is occasionally interpreted and applied as typical of the system, although it could also be interpreted and applied otherwise? If a modest degree of participation is not sufficient, what degree is? And how should it be determined in a way that satisfies legal certainty? These questions demonstrate that, below the threshold of extreme injustice, every denial of legal character incurs a serious loss of legal certainty. Rebuffing the principle of legal certainty is just barely tolerable in cases of extreme injustice; no further restriction of the principle is acceptable. This means, when legal character is at issue, that the criterion of extreme injustice is to be upheld and that this criterion is to be applied to individual norms and

only to individual norms. The extension thesis may be plausible in other contexts, but, as a thesis on legal character, it
cannot persuade. It cannot, therefore, lead to the conclusion
that the lawless or unjust character of a legal system as a
whole gives rise to consequences that go beyond the consequences of applying the argument from injustice to individual
norms.

The Collapse Thesis. The question now is whether the
second interpretation yields something else. Here, the statement that a system of norms forfeits its legal character if it is
by and large unjust in the extreme is interpreted in terms of
the collapse thesis, which, in contrast to the extension thesis,
asserts that only if an individual norm is itself unjust in the
extreme does it forfeit its legal character on grounds of morality. The collapse thesis is based, then, on the argument from
injustice applied to individual norms, as expressed in Radbruch's formula, and, with reference to individual norms,
nothing is added to that argument. The collapse thesis takes
the legal system as a whole into account in the assertion that
the system collapses as a legal system if very many individual
norms, in particular those important to the system, are denied
legal character. The reason for the collapse is not some sort of
extension or another, but, rather, the simple fact that there is
no longer enough left over to be called a legal system.

The collapse thesis is correct in asserting that the character
of a legal system can change fundamentally if very many of its
individual norms, in particular those important to the system,
are denied legal character. In this case, one can also speak of a
change in the contentual identity of the legal system and, in
this sense but only in this sense, of a collapse of the old
system. What is decisive here, however, is that in another
sense, focused not on contentual identity but on the existence
of a system as a legal system, a collapse is out of the question.
Even when a great many individual norms are denied legal
character on grounds of morality, including many that are
important to the character of the system, even then the system

can continue to exist as a legal system. This presupposes that a minimum complement of norms, the minimum necessary for the existence of a legal system, retain legal character. Take a legal system whose constitution empowers a dictator to issue norms without constraint. Thirty per cent of the norms issued by the dictator on the basis of this empowerment are unjust in the extreme, 20 per cent are unjust but not in the extreme, 20 per cent are neither unjust nor required by justice, and 30 per cent are required by justice. The 30 per cent that are unjust in the extreme are the norms that lend to the rogue system its specific character. The 30 per cent that are required by justice are, say, norms of contract law, tort law, and social security law. According to Radbruch's formula, legal character is to be denied only to that 30 per cent of norms that are unjust in the extreme. The formula does not apply to the remaining 70 per cent. Thus, the existence of the legal system would be endangered only if the 30 per cent of norms that are unjust in the extreme were to have such an effect on the empowering norm that, as a norm of extreme injustice, it forfeited its legal character over its entire range. For then the remaining 70 per cent of the norms of the system would also forfeit the basis of their validity. And then the legal system, as a hierarchically constructed system, would forfeit its existence and in this sense collapse. Only a partial class of norms could still be characterized as a system based on customary and/or natural law. That would be another system, though, in spite of the partial identity of the norms.

The latter makes clear that one would have to resort to relatively artificial constructions in denying legal character to an empowering norm over its entire range if on its basis extreme injustice can be or is being enacted. Legal norms duly issued on the basis of socially efficacious empowering norms would have to be classified as customary and/or natural law in order to explain their validity. That this is also unreasonable in its consequences becomes clear if one simply changes the dictator in the example into a democratically elected parliament that makes use, as described, of the empowerment to issue norms. Then the possible objection disappears that it is unjust in the extreme to empower one single person to issue norms without constraint. The empowering norm as such, given this presupposition, would not be unjust in the extreme. Only a partial class of its progeny is. That means, however, that the 30 per cent of norms that are unjust in the extreme do not lead to a forfeiture of legal character on the part of the empowering norm as such,[121] and the legal system as a whole does not collapse.

For the record, then: applying the argument from injustice to a legal system as a whole does not lead to consequences that go beyond the consequences of applying the argument to individual norms.[122]

(iii) The Argument from Principles

The argument from injustice focuses on an exceptional situation, that of the statute that is unjust in the extreme. The argument from principles is addressed to the everyday life of the law. Its point of departure is an insight of legal method agreed upon by positivists and non-positivists alike. As Hart puts it, every positive law has 'an open texture'.[123] There are several reasons for this. Of special significance are the vagaries

---

[121] It is typical that the Federal Constitutional Court, in its *Concordat* decision, does not mention the problem discussed here. Rather, it restricts itself to the inverse question, namely, whether all norms based on the Enabling Act of 24 March 1933 are necessarily to be seen as valid law. The Court answers in the negative: 'Simple recognition of the new system of competence says nothing about whether the statutes and ordinances issued on its basis can be recognized as valid law. For that, what is at issue is their *content*. They cannot be recognized as valid law if they contravene the essence and the possible content of the law.' *BVerfGE* 6 (1957), 309, at 331–2 (emphasis in original).

[122] The character of the legal system as a whole is of significance in a different respect, namely, that of the recognition of states and governments under international law. At issue here is the collision between the principles of effectiveness and legitimacy, with the former predominant in both the theory and the practice of such recognition. See e.g. Knut Ipsen, *Völkerrecht*, 3rd edn. (Munich: C. H. Beck, 1990), at 237.

[123] Hart, *CL* 124, 2nd edn. 128.

of legal language, the possibility of norm conflicts, the absence of a norm on which to base a decision, and, in certain cases, the possibility of making a decision even contrary to the literal reading of a norm.[124] One can speak here of an 'open area' of the positive law, which may be more or less broad, but which exists in every legal system. A case that falls within the open area shall be called a 'doubtful case'. From the standpoint of positivistic theory, this phenomenon can be interpreted in only one way. In the open area of the positive law, one cannot, by definition, base a decision on the positive law, for if one could do that, the case would not be in the open area. Since only the positive law is law, the judge must decide in the open area, that is, in all doubtful cases, on the basis of non-legal or extra-legal standards. Accordingly, he is empowered by the positive law to create new law essentially as a legislator does, on the basis of extra-legal standards.[125] Over a century ago, John Austin put it into words this way: 'So far as the judge's *arbitrium* extends, there is no law at all.'[126]

By contrast, the argument from principles says that the judge is legally bound even in the open area of the positive (issued and efficacious) law, indeed, legally bound in a way that establishes a necessary connection between law and morality.[127] This is reflected in the decision mentioned above in the context of judicial development of the law, where the Federal Constitutional Court says: 'The law is not identical

---

[124] Alexy, *TLA* 1.

[125] See e.g. Kelsen, *PTL*, at § 46 (pp. 353–5).

[126] Austin, *Lectures* vol. 2, 664 (Austin's emphasis).

[127] In this sense, see also Franz Bydlinski, *Juristische Methodenlehre und Rechtsbegriff* (Vienna and New York: Springer, 1982), at 289–90, who calls his argument a 'methodological argument'; similarly Ronald Dworkin, *Law's Empire* (Cambridge, Mass.: Harvard University Press, 1986), at 87, 410, who conceives of law in terms of interpretation: 'Law is an interpretive concept.' See Claudia Bittner, *Recht als interpretative Praxis* (Berlin: Duncker & Humblot, 1988), at 20–5; Marc Maria Strolz, *Ronald Dworkins These der Rechte im Vergleich zur gesetzgeberischen Methode nach Art. 1 Abs. 2 und 3 ZGB* (Zurich: Schulthess Polygraphischer Verlag, 1991), at 98–118.

with the totality of written statutes. As against the express directives of state authorities, there can be in some circumstances a greater law...'.[128]

The argument from principles is based on the distinction between rules and principles.[129] Rules are norms that, upon satisfaction of the conditions specified therein, prescribe a definitive legal consequence, that is, upon satisfaction of certain conditions, they definitively command, forbid, or permit something, or definitively confer power to some end or another. For simplicity's sake, rules may be called '*definitive commands*'. The characteristic form of their application is subsumption. By contrast, principles are *optimizing commands*. As such, they are norms commanding that something be realized to the greatest possible extent relative to the factual and legal possibilities at hand. This means that principles can be realized to varying degrees and that the commanded extent of their realization is dependent on not only factual potential but also legal potential. The legal possibilities for realizing a principle, besides being determined by rules, are essentially determined by competing principles, implying that principles can and must be balanced against one another. The characteristic form for applying principles is the balancing of one against another.

This theoretical distinction between norms as rules and as principles leads to a necessary connection between law and morality by way of three theses: the 'incorporation thesis', the 'morality thesis', and the 'correctness thesis'. The necessary connection that can be established with the help of these theses is, first, a conceptual connection, second, simply a qualifying connection, not—as the argument from injustice has it—a classifying connection, and it exists, third, only for a participant in the legal system, not for an observer of the legal system.

---

[128] *BVerfGE* 34 (1973), 269, at 287.
[129] On this theme, see Ronald Dworkin, *Taking Rights Seriously* (Cambridge, Mass.: Harvard University Press, 1977), at 14–45; Alexy, *TCR*, at 44–110; Jan-Reinard Sieckmann, *Regelmodelle und Prinzipienmodelle des Rechtssystems* (Baden-Baden: Nomos, 1990), at 52–87.

(a) The Incorporation Thesis

The *incorporation thesis* says that every legal system that is at least minimally developed necessarily comprises principles. In a fully developed legal system, such an incorporation is readily apparent, and the legal system of Germany offers an instructive example. The German Basic Law or Constitution, in affirming the principles of human dignity,[130] liberty,[131] equality,[132] the *Rechtsstaat* or rule of law, democracy, and the social state,[133] has incorporated into the German legal system, as principles of positive law, the basic principles of modern natural law and the law of reason and thereby the basic principles of modern legal and state morality. The same may be said of all legal systems affirming democracy and the *Rechtsstaat*, notwithstanding varying techniques for incorporating principles and different assessments of them.

No positivist will challenge this, provided he accepts that, alongside rules, principles can also belong to the legal system. What he will challenge, however, is that the result is some conceptually necessary connection between law and morality. Several arguments are available to him. One is that it is exclusively a question of positive law whether or not any principles at all are incorporated into a legal system.[134] Were this correct,

---

[130] *GG* art. 1, para. 1: 'Human dignity is inviolable. To respect and protect it is the duty of all state authority.'

[131] *GG* art. 2, para. 1: 'Everyone has the right to the free development of his personality in so far as he does not violate the rights of others or offend against the constitutional order or the moral law.'

[132] *GG* art. 3, para. 1: 'All persons are equal before the law.'

[133] *GG* art. 20, paras. 1–3: (1) 'The Federal Republic of Germany is a democratic and social federal state. (2) All state authority emanates from the people. It shall be exercised by the people through elections and voting and by specific legislative, executive, and judicial organs. (3) Legislation is subject to the constitutional order; the executive and the judiciary are bound by statute and law' (trans. altered). *GG*, art. 28, para. 1: 'The constitutional order in the *Länder* must conform to the principles of a republican, democratic, and social state under the rule of law, within the meaning of this Basic Law' (trans. altered).

[134] Hoerster, *LR* 186; Hoerster, *VR* 2481.

the argument from principles would be defeated in the very first round. It could at best still claim that a connection established by the positive law exists between law and morality. This would be compatible with legal positivism, for the positivist does not deny that the positive law, as Hoerster puts it, 'can guarantee that morality be taken into account'.[135] What the positivist does insist upon is simply that it is up to the positive law to decide whether or not morality is to play a role.

Is it, then, that not only some legal systems, on the basis of positive law, comprise norms structured like principles, but, rather, that all legal systems necessarily comprise norms structured like principles? This question shall be answered from the perspective of a participant, namely, a judge who is to decide a doubtful case, that is, a case that falls within the open area of the legal system and so cannot be decided on the basis of preset authoritative material alone. A criterion for whether or not the judge appeals to principles for support is whether or not he undertakes to strike a balance. The following proposition seems to be true: In undertaking to strike a balance, one necessarily appeals to principles for support. For it is necessary to strike a balance precisely when there are competing reasons, each of which is by itself a good reason for a decision and only fails to lead directly to a definitive decision because of the other reason, calling for another decision; reasons like this are either principles or supported by principles.[136]

---

[135] Hoerster, *LR* 186.

[136] Günther claims that the distinction between rules and principles ought not to be understood as a distinction between two types of norm, but, rather, solely as a distinction between two types of norm application. See Klaus Günther, *The Sense of Appropriateness*, trans. John Farrell (Albany, NY: State University of New York Press, 1993), at 212–19. By way of rejoinder, it should be pointed out that a model depicting the distinction between rules and principles at the level of norms as well as at the level of application is more comprehensive. Such a model can explain, for example, why a certain type of application takes place. In any case, one cannot forgo the distinction between rules and principles, for only with its help can one adequately reconstruct concepts like the concept of restricting a right. See Alexy, *TCR*, at 178–222.

A positivist can concede this point and still challenge the view that what follows from it is that principles are included in all legal systems in which judges undertake to strike a balance in doubtful cases. The positivist may claim that the simple fact that balancing is undertaken does not mean that the principles being balanced against one another belong to the legal system. They are simply moral principles, he may argue, or principles to be qualified in some other way, and the requirement of balancing one against another is an extra-legal postulate, not a legal one. A response in support of the argument from principles is that, for a participant, the legal system is not only a system of norms qua results or products, but also a system of procedures or processes, and so, from the participant's perspective, the reasons taken into account in a procedure—here, the process of making a decision and justifying it—belong to the procedure and thereby to the legal system.

An opponent of the argument from principles need not rest content with this point either. He may object that the simple fact that the judge takes into account certain reasons, namely, principles, in the process of making a decision and justifying it need not lead to the conclusion that they belong to the legal system. This objection can be dispelled, however, with the help of the argument from correctness. As explained above, a judicial decision necessarily lays claim to correctness.[137] This claim, because it is necessarily attached to the judicial decision, is a legal claim and not simply a moral one. Corresponding to this legal claim to correctness is a legal obligation to satisfy the claim, quite apart from the legal consequences of failing to do so. The claim to correctness requires, in a doubtful case, that whenever possible a balance be struck and thereby principles be taken into account. So the claim to correctness is necessarily unsatisfied if a judge, in a doubtful case, offers the following reason for choosing one of two decisions that are both compatible with the authoritative material: 'Had I struck a balance, I would have arrived at

[137] See above, this text, at 38–9.

the other decision, but I did not strike a balance.' This makes it clear that in all legal systems in which there are doubtful cases that give rise to the question of striking a balance, it is legally required to strike a balance and thereby to take principles into account. Thus, in all legal systems of this kind, principles are, for legal reasons, necessary elements of the legal system.

There is a last resort for the opponent of the argument from principles. He may claim that there can be legal systems in which no case is felt to be doubtful, so that in no case does the question of striking a balance arise. Since decisions can be made in such legal systems without taking principles into account, he may argue, it is not correct to say that all legal systems necessarily comprise norms structured like principles. I shall not pursue here the interesting empirical question of whether there have ever been legal systems in which no case was felt to be doubtful, so that in no case did the question of striking a balance arise. In any event, such a system would not even be a minimally developed legal system. Thus, the following proposition is true: Beginning at a minimum level of development, all legal systems necessarily comprise principles. This is a sufficient basis for establishing, by way of the argument from principles, a necessary connection between law and morality. The thesis that all legal systems necessarily comprise principles can therefore—without thereby defeating the argument from principles—be limited in accordance with the proposition above, namely, to legal systems that are at least minimally developed.

(b) The Morality Thesis

That all legal systems, beginning at a minimum level of development, necessarily comprise norms structured like principles is not enough to justify the conclusion that a necessary connection exists between law and morality. Such a connection is not yet established, then, by the simple fact, say, that the basic principles of modern legal and state morality are incorporated into all legal systems affirming democracy and the *Rechtsstaat*. Every positivist can say that the incorporation of precisely these principles is based on positive law. And that can be sharpened into the statement that it is always a question of the positive law whether or not principles belonging to a legal system establish a connection between law and morality.

In order to respond here, one must distinguish between two versions of the thesis of a necessary connection between law and morality: a weak and a strong version. In the weak version, the thesis says that a necessary connection exists between law and *some* morality. The strong version has it that a necessary connection exists between law and the *right* or *correct* morality. Here, only the weak version is of interest initially, that is, the thesis that the necessary presence of principles in the legal system leads to a necessary connection between law and some morality or another. This thesis shall be called the '*morality thesis*'.

The morality thesis is correct if, among the principles to be taken into account in doubtful cases in order to satisfy the claim to correctness, some principles are always found that belong to some morality or another. That is in fact so. In doubtful cases, the task is to find an answer to a practical question where an answer cannot be definitively drawn from the preset authoritative material. To answer a practical question in the legal arena is to say what is obligatory. One who wants to say what is obligatory but cannot support his answer exclusively by appeal to the decisions of an authority must take into account all relevant principles if he wants to satisfy the claim to correctness. But among the principles relevant to the solution of a practical question are always principles that belong to some morality or another. These need not be as abstract as the principles of liberty or the *Rechtsstaat*. Often, they are relatively concrete, as are the principles of non-retroactivity or environmental protection. In terms of content, too, some—say, the principle of racial segregation—

can be sharply distinguished from the principles of a democratic constitutional state. What is significant here is only that these principles are at the same time always principles of some morality or another, whether or not this morality be correct.

A positivist could object that this is not incompatible with his theory. Indeed, legal positivism emphasizes precisely the requirement that the judge decide in doubtful cases on the basis of extra-legal standards, a requirement that includes the decision based on moral principles.[138] This objection, however, misses the decisive point, which is that principles, first, according to the incorporation thesis, are necessarily components of the legal system and, second, according to the morality thesis, necessarily include principles that belong to a morality. This dual quality of necessarily belonging at the same time to law and to morality means that the judge's decision in doubtful cases is to be interpreted otherwise than in positivistic theories. Principles that are, according to their content, moral principles are incorporated into the law, so that the judge who appeals to them for support is making his decision on the basis of legal standards. Calling on the ambiguous dichotomy of form and content, one can say that, according to form, the judge's decision is based on legal reasons, but, according to content, it is based on moral reasons.

(c) The Correctness Thesis

What has been shown so far is simply that the argument from principles leads to a necessary connection between law and some kind of morality. The obvious objection is that this is too little. For when one speaks of a necessary connection between law and morality, one generally means a necessary connection between law and the—or a—correct morality.

---

[138] See Hart, *CL*, at 199, 2nd edn., at 203–4: 'The law of every modern state shows at a thousand points the influence of both the accepted social morality and wider moral ideals.'

That is especially true from the participant's perspective. This objection would in fact undermine the non-positivist if the argument from principles were not successful in establishing some kind of a necessary connection between law and correct morality. That the argument does succeed in establishing just such a connection is the substance of the *correctness thesis*. The correctness thesis is the result of applying the argument from correctness within the framework of the argument from principles.

The correctness thesis presents no problems if the content of principles of positive law is morally required or at least morally permitted. An example would be the six basic principles of the German Basic Law or Constitution, namely, the principles of human dignity, liberty, equality, the *Rechtsstaat* or rule of law, democracy, and the social state. As optimizing commands, these principles require realization to the greatest possible extent. Together they require a realization that approximates a legal ideal, namely, the ideal of the democratic, social *Rechtsstaat*.[139] If these principles or their numerous subprinciples are relevant in a doubtful case, then the judge is legally obligated to undertake an optimal realization of them, geared to the concrete case. He is to answer a legal question that, according to its content, is also a question of political morality. At least some of the arguments with which the judge justifies the balance he strikes have, in terms of content, the character of moral arguments. It follows, then, that the claim to legal correctness necessarily attached to the decision includes a claim to moral correctness. Therefore, in legal systems whose positive law principles have a content that is morally required or at least morally permitted, a necessary connection exists between law and correct morality.

An opponent of the argument from principles may object that this leads to a necessary connection between law and correct morality only in morally vindicated legal systems,

---

[139] Ralf Dreier, *Rechtsbegriff und Rechtsidee* (Frankfurt: Alfred Metzner, 1986), 30–1.

not, however, to a quintessential necessary connection that applies to all legal systems. He may refer in this context to a legal system like that of National Socialism, which, with its principles of race and absolute leadership (the *Führer*-principle),[140] comprised principles reflecting a morality altogether different from that reflected by the principles of the German Basic Law. How is it that here, he may ask, the application of the argument from correctness within the framework of the argument from principles is supposed to lead to a necessary connection between law and correct morality?

It does not matter at this point that here the argument from principles meets the argument from injustice. What is decisive is that even the judge who applies the principle of race and the *Führer*-principle lays claim to correctness with his decision. The claim to correctness implies a *claim to justifiability*. This claim is not limited to the justifiability of the decision in terms of some kind of morality leading to the correctness of the decision; rather, it refers to the correctness of the decision in terms of a justifiable and therefore correct morality. The necessary connection between law and correct morality is established in that the claim to correctness includes a claim to moral correctness that also applies to the principles on which the decision is based.

A critic could object that in this way the link between law and correct morality is so dissipated that one can no longer speak of a necessary connection. The concern now is only with a claim and no longer with its satisfaction, and, in addition, despite the emphasis on correct morality, there is no talk of what correct morality is. Both of these observations

---

[140] See e.g. Wilhelm Stuckart and Hans Globke, *Kommentare zur deutschen Rassengesetzgebung*, vol. 1 (Munich and Berlin: C. H. Beck, 1936), at 7: 'The responsible leaders of the state are to examine the racial composition of the people entrusted to them and are to undertake due measures preventing at least the further loss of the best racial values and strengthening as much as possible the ethnic core.' And, at 13: 'From the idea of race flows inevitably the idea of the *Führer*. Thus, the ethnic national state must of necessity be a *Führer*-state.'

are correct, but they do not spell the downfall of the connection thesis.

It is easy to see that, outside the realm of the argument from injustice, that is, below the threshold of extreme injustice, the claim alone and not its satisfaction can establish a necessary connection between law and correct morality. To focus on the satisfaction of the claim is to say too much. It is to say that the law, including every single judicial decision, necessarily satisfies the claim to moral correctness, in short, that the law is always morally correct. The latter implies that whatever is not morally correct is not law. A thesis that strong cannot be defended, as shown in the discussion of the argument from injustice. Thus, the issue here cannot be a classifying connection, it can only be a qualifying connection. Below the threshold of extreme injustice, a violation of morality means not that the norm or decision in question forfeits legal character, in other words, is not law (a classifying connection), but, rather, that the norm or decision in question is legally defective (a qualifying connection). The claim to correctness that is necessarily attached to the law, because it includes a claim to moral correctness, is the reason that, below the threshold of extreme injustice, a violation of correct morality leads not, indeed, to the forfeiture of legal character, but necessarily to legal defectiveness. The classifying connection can be called 'hard', the qualifying connection, 'soft'. Even soft connections can be necessary.

The remaining objection is that simply referring to correct morality is too little. This objection cannot be dispelled by providing a comprehensive system of moral rules that permit in every case a certain judgment about whether or not these rules are being violated by a legal norm or a judicial decision. Beyond the threshold of extreme injustice, there is broad agreement about what violates morality, but below this threshold, controversy prevails. This does not mean that, below the threshold, there are no standards whatsoever for what is just and what is unjust. The key is the claim to justifiability implicit in the claim to correctness. The claim to justifiability leads to requirements that must be satisfied at a minimum by morality in order that this morality not be identified as false morality, and it leads to requirements that must be satisfied to the greatest possible extent by morality in order that this morality stand a chance of being the—or a— correct morality.[141] An example of the failure to satisfy these requirements is the justification of the principle of race as set out in the 1936 commentary of Stuckart and Globke:

> Based on the most rigorous scientific examination, we know today that the human being, to the deepest unconscious stirrings of his temperament, but also to the smallest fibril of his brain, exists in the reality and the inescapability of his ethnic and racial origins. Race stamps his spiritual countenance no less than his outward form. It determines his thoughts and sensibilities, his strengths and propensities, it constitutes his particular character, his nature.[142]

This justification does not satisfy the minimum requirements of a rational justification. Consider only the claim that race determines the thoughts of the individual. Far from reflecting 'the most rigorous scientific examination', this claim is empirically false, which the most quotidian of experience demonstrates.

The qualifying or soft connection that emerges when the legal system is considered as a system of procedures, too, from the perspective of a participant leads not to a necessary connection between law and a particular morality to be labelled as correct in terms of content, but, rather, to a necessary connection between law and the idea of correct morality as a justified morality. This idea is far from empty. Linking it with the law means that not only are the special rules of juridical justification part of the law, but the general rules of moral argumentation are too, for whatever correctness is possible in the area of morality is possible on the basis of these rules. They thwart considerable irrationality and injustice. What is

---

[141] See Alexy, *TLA*, at 187–205.
[142] Stuckart and Globke, *Kommentare zur deutschen Rassengesetzgebung* (n. 140 above), 10.

more, the idea of correct morality has the character of a
regulative idea in the sense of a goal to be pursued.[143] Thus,
the claim to correctness leads to an ideal dimension that is
necessarily linked with the law.

[143] See Immanuel Kant, *Critique of Pure Reason* (1st pub. 1781, 2nd edn.
1787), trans. and ed. Paul Guyer and Allen W. Wood (Cambridge: Cambridge University Press, 1997), at A644/B672 (p. 591) (trans. altered): 'On
the contrary, transcendental ideas have an excellent and indispensably
necessary regulative use, namely, that of directing the understanding
toward a certain goal, the prospect of which has the directional lines of all
its rules converging into one point.'

III

The Validity of Law

1. Concepts of Validity

Corresponding to the three elements of the concept of law—the elements of social efficacy, correctness of content, and authoritative issuance—are three concepts of validity: the sociological, the ethical, and the juridical.

A. THE SOCIOLOGICAL CONCEPT OF VALIDITY

The subject-matter of the sociological concept of validity is social validity. A norm is valid *socially* if it is complied with or a sanction is imposed for non-compliance. This definition allows for numerous interpretations. One reason it does is that the concepts employed in the definition—the concepts of compliance and the imposition of a sanction for non-compliance—are ambiguous. This is especially true of the concept of compliance with a norm. One may ask, say, whether it is sufficient for compliance with a norm that behaviour conform externally to the norm, or whether compliance with a norm presupposes certain knowledge and motives on the part of the complying person. If one focuses on the latter, one faces the question of what knowledge and which motives must be present before one can speak of compliance with a norm. The second reason the definition of social validity allows for numerous interpretations is that a norm may be complied with to varying degrees, and the imposition of a sanction for non-compliance may also vary in degree. The result is that the social efficacy of a norm and thereby its social validity is a matter of degree. A norm with a high degree of efficacy is complied with in, say, 80 per cent of the situations in which it is applicable, and a sanction is imposed in, say, 95 per cent of the cases of non-compliance. By contrast, the degree of efficacy is very low for a norm that is complied with in, say, merely 5 per cent of the situations in which it is applicable, and where a sanction is imposed in, say, merely 3 per cent of the cases of non-compliance. Between these extremes, however, the matter is less clear. Consider two norms, a norm at an 85 per cent level of compliance, but where a sanction is imposed in merely 1 per cent of the cases of non-compliance, and a norm at a mere 20 per cent level of compliance, but where a sanction is imposed in 98 per cent of the cases of non-compliance. The question of which of these two norms has a higher degree of social efficacy cannot be answered on the basis of the percentages alone. Any answer presupposes a determination, within the framework of the concept of social validity, of the relative significance of, on the one hand, compliance and, on the other, the imposition of a sanction for non-compliance.

The problems of social validity are thoroughly discussed in the field of legal sociology,[144] where empirical questions raised in the research into effectiveness[145] require a more precise statement. For our purposes here, three insights suffice. The first is that social validity is a matter of degree. The second is that social validity is recognizable with the help of two criteria: that of compliance and that of the imposition of a sanction for non-compliance. The third insight is that the imposition of a sanction for non-compliance with legal norms includes the exercise of physical coercion, which, in developed legal systems, is a task reserved to the state.[146]

---

[144] See Hubert Rottleuthner, *Rechtstheorie und Rechtssoziologie* (Freiburg and Munich: Karl Alber, 1981), at 91–115; Klaus F. Röhl, *Rechtssoziologie* (Cologne *et al.*: Carl Heymann, 1987), at 243–51.

[145] See Hubert Rottleuthner, *Einführung in die Rechtssoziologie* (Darmstadt: Wissenschaftliche Buchgesellschaft, 1987), at 54–77.

[146] See above, this text, at 14–15.

B. The Ethical Concept of Validity

The subject-matter of the ethical concept of validity is moral validity. A norm is valid *morally* if it is morally justified. An ethical concept of validity underlies the theories of natural law and the law of reason. The validity of a norm of natural law or a norm of the law of reason rests neither on its social efficacy nor on its authoritative issuance, but, rather, solely on the correctness of its content, to be demonstrated by moral justification.

C. The Juridical Concept of Validity

The sociological and the ethical concepts of validity are pure in the sense that they need not necessarily include elements of the other concepts of validity. It is different for the juridical concept of validity. Its subject-matter is legal validity. If a norm or a system of norms is not socially valid at all, that is, fails to manifest the slightest social efficacy, then this norm or system of norms cannot be legally valid either. The concept of legal validity necessarily includes, then, elements of social validity. If it includes only elements of social validity, it is a positivistic concept of legal validity, whereas if it also comprises elements of moral validity, it is a non-positivistic concept of legal validity.

The fact that a fully developed concept of legal validity qua positivistic concept includes elements of social validity and qua non-positivistic concept includes elements of both social and moral validity does not preclude the formation of a *concept of legal validity in a narrower sense*. Such a concept refers exclusively to specific characteristics of legal validity and is, then, a concept in contrast to the concepts of social and moral validity. Such a concept of legal validity is reflected in the statement that a norm is *legally* valid if it has been issued in the duly prescribed way by a duly authorized organ and does not violate higher-ranking law, in short, if it is authoritatively issued.

The juridical concept of validity poses two problems, an internal and an external problem. The internal problem is that the definition of legal validity seems to be circular in that it presupposes legal validity at the outset. How else should one say what a 'duly authorized organ' is or what the issuance of a norm 'in the duly prescribed way' amounts to? This internal problem leads to the problem of the basic norm. The external problem lies in determining how the juridical concept of validity is related to both of the other concepts of validity. The relation to the ethical concept of validity has been discussed above in the context of legal positivism, the relation to the sociological concept of validity is still outstanding. The external problem will be aired here first, in the course of which, for systematic reasons, the relation of the juridical concept of validity to the ethical concept of validity will be taken up once again.

2. Collisions of Validity

Extreme cases enable one to see what is scarcely visible in ordinary situations. For concepts of validity, the extreme cases are collisions of validity. The collision of legal and social validity will be our first concern.

A. LEGAL AND SOCIAL VALIDITY

It has been shown above that what applies to a system of norms need not necessarily apply to an individual norm. Systems of norms alone, then, will be considered first.

(i) Systems of Norms

A condition for the legal validity of a system of norms is that the norms belonging to the system be *by and large* socially efficacious, that is, socially valid.[147] Only developed legal systems will be considered here. The legal validity of the norms of a developed legal system rests on a written or unwritten constitution that states the conditions under which a norm belongs to the legal system and therefore is legally valid. The mere fact that individual norms that are legally valid according to constitutional criteria for validity lose their social validity does not by itself mean that the constitution, and with it its system of norms as a whole, forfeits legal validity. This threshold is crossed only if the norms belonging to the system of norms are no longer by

[147] See Kelsen, *PTL* § 34(g) (at pp. 212–13).

and large socially efficacious, that is, are no longer by and large complied with or a sanction is no longer by and large imposed for non-compliance.

The question of the validity of a system of norms as a whole is posed with greatest clarity where two incompatible systems of norms compete. This situation may arise, say, in the case of a revolution, a civil war, or a secession. It is easy to say what is valid following the victory of one party or the other. Then, the system of norms that has prevailed against the other system is valid, for its prevailing means that it is now the only system of norms that is by and large socially efficacious. It is not so easy to say what is valid during the competition between the systems of norms, that is, during the political struggle. There are three possibilities. The first is that neither of the two systems of norms is valid as a system of norms, because neither is by and large socially efficacious. The second possibility is that the system of norms victorious in the end is already valid, although no one knows yet which system this will be. The third possibililty is that the old system of norms, although it is no longer by and large efficacious, is valid until the new system of norms has prevailed, that is, is by and large socially efficacious. A theory of the changing from one legal system to another is charged with the study of these possibilities as well as of numerous intermediate forms.

According to Hoerster, a characteristic of the concept of law is that a system of norms is a legal system, or is legally valid, only if it 'prevails in the event of open conflict with other normative coercive systems in the society'.[148] This criterion may be called the 'dominance criterion'. The dominance criterion, because it is contained in the criterion that a system of norms be by and large socially efficacious, adds nothing to that criterion. A system of norms that fails to prevail against other normative coercive systems is not by and large socially efficacious.

---

[148] Hoerster, *LR* 184.

(ii) Individual Norms

An authoritatively issued norm of a legal system that is by and large socially efficacious does not forfeit its legal validity simply because it is frequently not complied with and a sanction is only rarely imposed for non-compliance. Unlike legal systems, individual norms need not be by and large socially efficacious as a condition for legal validity. It is easy to see the reason for this difference. One may say of an individual norm that it is valid because it belongs to a legal system that is by and large socially efficacious. To say the same thing of a legal system, which could belong to no other legal system than itself, makes no sense.

There is, nevertheless, for individual norms, too, a relation between legal and social validity that can have consequences for legal validity in the event of a collision between the two. A condition for the legal validity of an individual norm is not, to be sure, that the norm be by and large socially efficacious, but, rather, that the norm exhibit a *minimum social efficacy or prospect of social efficacy*. Corresponding to this is the phenomenon of derogation through customary law (*desuetudo*), which consists in the forfeiture of the legal validity of a norm owing to a decline in the efficacy of the norm to a level below the minimum. Like the standard requiring that legal systems be by and large socially efficacious, this minimum for individual norms cannot in general—that is, apart from the case of complete inefficacy—be stipulated exactly. Thus, there can be cases where it is highly uncertain whether or not a norm has forfeited its legal validity owing to a derogation through customary law.

B. Legal and Moral Validity

The collision between legal and moral validity has been covered above in the context of the critique of positivistic concepts of law.[149] The sole concern here, then, is to compare

---

[149] See above, this text, at 20–81.

the results of that enquiry with the resolution of the collision between legal and social validity.

(i) Systems of Norms

A system of norms that neither explicitly nor implicitly lays claim to correctness is not a legal system and therefore cannot be legally valid. This has few practical consequences, for actually existing legal systems regularly lay claim to correctness, however feebly justified the claim may be.

Practically speaking, significant problems first turn up where the claim to correctness is indeed made, but remains unsatisfied to such a degree that the system of norms is classified an unjust or a lawless system (*Unrechtssystem*). The issue then is the application of the argument from injustice to a system of norms as a whole. It appears on first glance that a usable formula might correspond to the one used in resolving the collision between legal and social validity, that is, to say here that a system of norms forfeits its legal validity if it is by and large unjust in the extreme. The discussion of the extension and the collapse theses has shown, however, that this solution is out of the question.[150] Application of the argument from injustice is limited to individual norms. Only when, owing to the argument from injustice, legal character is denied to so many individual norms that there is no longer a minimum complement of norms, the minimum necessary for the existence of a legal system, only then does the system cease to exist as a legal system. That is not, however, a consequence of applying the argument from injustice to the legal system as a whole, but a consequence of the consequences of applying the argument from injustice to individual norms. As for legal systems, there is an asymmetry between the relation of legal and social validity and the relation of legal and moral validity in that the legal validity of a legal system as a whole depends more on social validity than on moral validity. A legal system

---

[150] See above, this text, at 62–8.

that is not by and large socially efficacious collapses as a legal system. By contrast, a legal system may continue to exist as a legal system although it is by and large not morally justifiable. It collapses only when legal character and thereby legal validity is denied to so many individual norms because of extreme injustice that there is no longer a minimum complement of norms, the minimum necessary for the existence of a legal system.

An adequate concept of law turns on the relation of three elements to one another—authoritative issuance, social efficacy, and correctness of content.[151] It is now clear that authoritative issuance must be joined by social efficacy and correctness of content not in a general, equally weighted relation but, rather, in an ordered, hierarchical relation.

(ii) Individual Norms

Individual norms forfeit their legal character and thereby their legal validity if they are unjust in the extreme. In its structure, this criterion corresponds to the formula that an individual norm forfeits its legal validity if it fails to exhibit a minimum social efficacy or prospect of social efficacy.[152] Both statements focus on a limiting case. Instead of saying that an individual norm must exhibit a minimum social efficacy or prospect of social efficacy, one could say that the norm may not be extremely inefficacious socially or have a very slight prospect of social efficacy. Conversely, the formula that a norm forfeits legal validity if it is unjust in the extreme could be replaced with the formula that a condition for the legal validity of an individual norm is that the norm exhibit a minimum moral justifiability.[153] The latter admittedly invites misinterpretation. Even if a norm is simply unjust but not in the extreme, it still lacks a minimum moral justifiability, for an unjust norm as such cannot be justified and therefore

---

[151] See above, this text, at 13.
[152] See above, this text, at 91.
[153] See Ralf Dreier, 'Recht und Moral', in *RMI* 180–216, at 198.

cannot be justified to a marginal extent either. Nevertheless, a norm that is simply unjust can be legally valid. According to the formula focused on a minimum, however, this presupposes that the norm exhibit a minimum moral justifiability. The contradiction here can be resolved by applying the concept of a minimum moral justifiability not to individual norms as such, but to their legal validity. Because there are moral advantages to the existence of a legal system, the legal validity of a norm belonging to the system can exhibit a minimum moral justifiability even if the norm by itself, being unjust, does not do this. Thus, when the formula that focuses on a minimum is applied to moral justifiability, it presupposes complicated deliberations, giving the advantage to the straightforward criterion of extreme injustice.

The conclusion, then, is that the respective roles of social and moral validity within the framework of the concept of legal validity are structurally the same in terms of individual norms. In both, the focus is on a limiting case alone, giving expression to the fact that authoritative issuance within the framework of a socially efficacious legal system is the dominant criterion for the validity of individual norms. This conclusion is borne out every day in the work of the jurist.

3. Basic Norm

A concept of legal validity that leaves out the elements of social efficacy and correctness of content was classified above as a concept of legal validity in a narrower sense. It was noted that this concept poses two problems. Alongside an external problem that lies in determining how the concept of legal validity is related to social and moral validity, there is an internal problem, too.[154] The internal problem is the circularity of the definition of legal validity, which says that a norm is legally valid if it has been issued in the duly prescribed way by a duly authorized organ and does not violate higher-ranking law, in short, if it is authoritatively issued. The concepts of the duly authorized organ, issuance of a norm in the duly prescribed way, and higher-ranking law, however, all presuppose at the outset the concept of legal validity. They can only mean: an organ authorized on the basis of legally valid norms, issuance of a norm in a legally regulated way, and legally valid higher-ranking law. Otherwise this would not be about the concept of legal validity in a narrower sense.

The basic norm is the most significant instrument for resolving the circularity of the concept of legal validity in a narrower sense. Notwithstanding a great variety of possibilities for differentiation, three kinds of basic norm can be distinguished: analytical, normative, and empirical. The most important variant of the analytical basic norm is found in Hans Kelsen's legal theory, of the normative basic norm, in Kant's theory, and of the empirical basic norm, in H. L. A. Hart's theory.

---

[154] See above, this text, at 88.

A. The Analytical Basic Norm (Kelsen)

(i) Concept

A basic norm is a norm that is the basis for the validity of all the norms of a legal system, excepting its own validity. To arrive at the basic norm, one need only ask 'why' a few times around. Kelsen compares the gangster's command that a certain sum of money be handed over to him and the tax official's directive that the same sum be paid.[155] Why is the tax official's directive a legally valid individual norm[156] in the form of an administrative act, but, by contrast, the gangster's command is not? The answer is that the tax official can appeal to a statutory empowerment, but the gangster cannot. Why are the statutes supporting the tax official valid? The answer is that the constitution empowers the legislator to enact statutes like the empowerment of the tax official. But why is the constitution valid? One could say, here, that the constitution is valid because it has in fact been issued and is socially efficacious, and then go on to assert that this is the last stop and there is nothing more to say. If that were correct, then the norms of the constitution that empower the legislator to issue norms would be the—inherently complex—basic norm.

The problem with this answer is that it includes a transition from 'is' to 'ought'. The 'is' consists in the factual issuance and social efficacy of the constitution, which can be expressed in the statement,[157]

(2) Constitution *C* has in fact been issued and is socially efficacious.

The 'ought' is the legal validity of the constitution, which can be expressed in the statement,

(3′) Constitution *C* is legally valid.

---

[155] See Kelsen, *PTL* § 4(b) (at p. 8).

[156] On the concept of the individual norm, see Alexy, *TCR*, at 46.

[157] The reason for the non-sequential numbering here will become clear with the construction of the basic norm syllogism, below.

Statement (3′) is an 'ought'-statement, for it implies the statement,[158]

(3) It is legally prescribed that one behave in accordance with constitution *C*.

But not one single normative statement ever follows *logically*[159] from an 'is',[160] more precisely, from any class whatsoever of exclusively empirical statements. So to go from (2) to (3) or (3′), an additional premiss is needed. This additional premiss is the *basic norm*. It can be so formulated that either it permits the move from (2) to (3′)—(3) is then to be derived from (3′)—or it leads directly to (3). The latter formulation will be considered here. It reads,

(1) If a constitution has in fact been issued and is socially efficacious, then it is legally prescribed that one behave in accordance with this constitution.

---

[158] See Kelsen, *PTL* § 34(a) (at p. 193).

[159] It should be emphasized that the issue here is logical deducibility. The expression 'follows' is often used, albeit incorrectly, to say that something is a good reason for something else. Empirical statements can of course serve as good reasons for normative statements. But then a normative premiss is always presupposed that turns the empirical statements into good reasons.

[160] The thesis that no 'ought' follows from an 'is' alone can be traced back to Hume, and so it is also called 'Hume's Law'. See David Hume, *A Treatise of Human Nature* (1st pub. 1739–40), ed. David Fate Norton and Mary J. Norton (Oxford: Oxford University Press, 2000), bk. III, pt. 1, sect. 1, para. 27 (at p. 302) (emphasis in original): 'In every system of morality, which I have hitherto met with, I have always remark'd, that the author proceeds for some time in the ordinary way of reasoning, and establishes the being of a God, or makes observations concerning human affairs; when of a sudden I am surpriz'd to find, that instead of the usual copulations of propositions, *is*, and *is not*, I meet with no proposition that is not connected with an *ought*, or an *ought not*. This change is imperceptible; but is, however, of the last consequence. For as this *ought*, or *ought not*, expresses some new relation or affirmation, 'tis necessary that it shou'd be observ'd and explain'd; and at the same time that a reason shou'd be given, for what seems altogether inconceivable, how this new relation can be a deduction from the others, which are entirely different from it.' For a statement on the logical questions arising from the 'is'–'ought' distinction, see Rainer Stuhlmann-Laeisz, *Das Sein-Sollen-Problem* (Stuttgart–Bad Cannstatt: Frommann-Holzboog, 1983).

The statements (1), (2), and (3) can now be brought together in a *basic norm syllogism* that has the following form:

(1) If a constitution has in fact been issued and is socially efficacious, then it is legally prescribed that one behave in accordance with this constitution.

(2) Constitution *C* has in fact been issued and is socially efficacious.

(3) It is legally prescribed that one behave in accordance with constitution *C*.[161]

Scarcely any other idea in legal theory has stirred up as much strife as the idea of a basic norm. The debate is concentrated on four points: the necessity, the possibility, the content, and the status of the basic norm.

(ii) Necessity

Hart's objection to the necessity of a basic norm is that it leads to unnecessary duplication.

If a constitution specifying the various sources of law is a living reality in the sense that the courts and officials of the system actually identify the law in accordance with the criteria it provides, then the constitution is accepted and actually exists. It seems a needless

---

[161] See Kelsen, *PTL* § 34(g) (at p. 212). Kelsen's basic norm syllogism is distinguishable in four respects from the syllogism formulated here. Three of these are insignificant, one is significant. That Kelsen formulates the basic norm categorically is insignificant: 'One ought to behave in accordance with a constitution that has in fact been issued and is efficacious', ibid. (trans. altered). This statement can, without any change in content, be reformulated hypothetically, as at (1) above, that is, in 'if'–'then' form. Insignificant, too, is the fact that, in Kelsen's formulation, the conclusion, at (3) above, refers not only to the constitution but to the entire legal system. Kelsen is simply going a step further thereby, a step that is not taken here but could be taken without difficulty. Finally, it is also insignificant that Kelsen uses the formulation 'one ought' and not the formulation 'is prescribed', as in (1) and (3) above. By contrast, it is significant that Kelsen says simply 'one ought', when in fact the point here is that something is '*legally* prescribed'. I return to this below.

reduplication to suggest that there is a further rule to the effect that the constitution (or those who 'laid it down') are to be obeyed.[162]

This is a powerful objection in that it does not apply the basic norm to things like expressions of will, behavioural patterns, and coercive measures that, with the help of the basic norm, are interpreted as a legally valid constitution, but, rather, focuses immediately on the institutional fact of a working constitution. Accordingly, the following statement could serve as the sole premiss of a justification of the legal 'ought':

(2′) The participants in legal system S accept and implement constitution C.

The question is whether this premiss implies the conclusion of the basic norm syllogism, namely:

(3) It is legally prescribed that one behave in accordance with constitution C.

An answer in the affirmative calls for the following interpretation of (3):

(3″) From the standpoint of a participant in legal system S, this is true: It is legally prescribed that one behave in accordance with constitution C.

The sentence (3″) follows from (2′) because the fact that the participants in a legal system accept and implement a constitution means that, from their standpoint, it is legally prescribed that one behave in accordance with this constitution. Is the basic norm rendered thereby superfluous? Is Alf Ross's rhetorical question on the mark? 'But the norm itself, according to its immediate content, expresses what the individual ought to do. What, then, is the meaning of saying that the individuals ought to do what they ought to do!'[163] The answer is 'no, the basic norm is not rendered superfluous'. The decisive point is that one may indeed be able to move from (2′) to (3″)

[162] Hart, *CL* 246, 2nd edn. 293.
[163] Alf Ross, *Directives and Norms* (London: Routledge & Kegan Paul, 1968), 156.

without the help of a basic norm, but (2′) itself presupposes a basic norm. That the participants in a legal system accept and implement a constitution presupposes that every single one of them interprets certain facts as facts creating the constitution. That may well amount to a very complex bundle of facts. Here, the variety will be reduced to two things, namely, that the constitution has been passed by a constitutional assembly and that the other participants in the legal system accept and implement the constitution. Take now a participant in legal system *S* who accepts and implements constitution *C*. This participant is questioned as to why constitution *C* is legally valid, which includes the question of why it is legally prescribed that one behave in accordance with constitution *C*.

The participant could try to evade the question by claiming that it is senseless. He could elaborate by asserting, with Hart, that those rules of the constitution that say what valid law is (Hart terms them collectively the 'rule of recognition') cannot in turn be said to be legally valid themselves. They are pre-supposed as existing, and their existence is 'a matter of fact'.[164] A response to that, however, is that the question as to the legal validity of a constitution is both possible and routine. It seems strange and artificial for a judge, asked why he follows the constitution, to answer, 'I follow the constitution not because it is legally valid, but exclusively because my colleagues and I accept and implement it. That is a matter of fact, and there is nothing more to say.' It is safe to assume, therefore, that the participant does not dismiss as senseless the question as to the legal validity of the constitution. Then his answer could run:

(2″) Constitution *C* was passed by the constitutional assembly, and the other participants in the legal system accept and implement it.

This statement is nothing other than a concretization of the second premiss in Kelsen's basic norm syllogism, namely,

---

[164] Hart, *CL* 107, 2nd edn. 110.

(2) Constitution *C* has in fact been issued and is socially efficacious.

But (2) alone implies neither the statement,

(3′) Constitution *C* is legally valid,

nor the statement,

(3) It is legally prescribed that one behave in accordance with constitution *C*.

In order to move from (2) or (2″) to (3′) or (3), a basic norm like (1) must be presupposed. A move from either (2) or (2″) alone to either (3′) or (3) is no more possible than a move from the statement (5) alone,

(5) Peter wants me to give him 100 marks,

to the conclusion,

(6) I am obligated to give Peter 100 marks.

What is needed in order to make the respective moves possible is, in the first case, the basic norm as introduced above, and, in the second case, a norm like

(4) I am obligated to do what Peter wants me to do.

There is no unnecessary duplication even if there is, from the issuer of a norm, not only an expression of will but, explicitly, the formulation of a norm. Assuming that Peter is speaking on his own authority—that is, without reference to law, morality, or social convention—when he declares that I am obligated to give him 100 marks, then (5′) alone,

(5′) Peter said to me, 'You are obligated to give me 100 marks',

does not imply

(6) I am obligated to give Peter 100 marks.

If it did, then words alone could establish any obligations whatsoever for any persons whatsoever. To arrive at (6) from (5′), a norm like (4′) is needed:

(4′) I am obligated to do whatever Peter says I am obligated to do.

This is duplication, but not unnecessary duplication.

The conclusion, then, is that there are two settled theses.
The first thesis states that if the participant in a legal system
wants to say that the constitution is legally valid or that it is
legally prescribed that one behave in accordance with the
constitution, then he must presuppose a basic norm. The
second thesis states that if the enquiry into legal validity is
not to be cut off arbitrarily, then it must be possible for the
participant to say that the constitution is legally valid or that
it is legally prescribed that one behave in accordance with the
constitution—which presupposes a basic norm.

(iii) Possibility

Not only can an opponent of the basic norm make the claim
just refuted, namely, that a basic norm is superfluous, he can
also object that the validity or the existence of a basic norm is
impossible. So it is that Ronald Dworkin countered Hart's
basic norm (rule of recognition) by maintaining that the law
cannot be identified on the basis of a rule that focuses on
authoritative issuance and social efficacy.[165] This objection
corresponds to the argument from principles set out above,[166]
according to which the law also includes the totality of the
standards that must be taken into account in order to satisfy
the claim to correctness that is necessarily attached to the law.
Indeed, these standards cannot be completely identified on the
basis of a rule that focuses on authoritative issuance and
social efficacy.

Nevertheless, the argument from principles does not dispose of the possibililty of a basic norm. It shows simply that a
basic norm that focuses only on empirically ascertainable

---

[165] See Dworkin, *Taking Rights Seriously* (n. 129 above), at 39–45, 64–8.
[166] See above, this text, at 68–81.

facts (issuance, efficacy) cannot identify the law completely. What a basic norm like this can identify, however, is authoritatively issued and socially efficacious law. The basic norm is to be interpreted, then, to the effect that authoritative issuance together with social efficacy is simply a sufficient condition for belonging to the law, not a necessary one. So, on the basis of the argument from principles, the following statement is not true:

(1) The law includes *everything* that has been authoritatively issued and is socially efficacious—*and nothing more*.

Rather, the weaker statement is true:

(2) The law includes *everything* that has been authoritatively issued and is socially efficacious.

As will be shown in the next section, even this statement requires a still weaker formulation if the argument from injustice[167] is to be taken into account. Within the framework of statement (2), however, a basic norm is not only possible, it is also necessary, namely, in order to be able to move from empirically ascertainable facts to legal validity.

A basic norm limited to authoritatively issued and socially efficacious law has the disadvantage of not being a complete, supreme identifying criterion for the law. This role can be recovered by the basic norm, not completely, but in limited terms. To that end, clauses must be added to it that take into account the arguments from injustice and from principles. Only the argument from principles is of interest at this point. Building the results of that argument into the basic norm yields a non-positivistic basic norm with the following structure:

If a constitution has in fact been issued and is socially efficacious, then it is legally prescribed that one behave in accordance with this constitution in such a way as corresponds to the claim to correctness.

---

[167] See above, this text, at 40–62.

This formulation shows that a non-positivistic basic norm has only limited usefulness in identifying the law. The clause, 'in such a way as corresponds to the claim to correctness', refers to moral standards without naming them and without mentioning any criterion whereby they can be unequivocally identified. This openness is unavoidable. It is acceptable only because there are rules of legal method that preclude allowing openness to lead to arbitrariness.[168] In particular, these rules prevent issued and efficacious norms from being arbitrarily suppressed by appeal to the claim to correctness.[169] They must do that, if for no other reason than that legal certainty is an essential element of legal correctness.

(iv) Content

According to Kelsen, the basic norm is entirely neutral in terms of content.

The question is not what the content is of this constitution and the state legal system erected on its basis, whether this system is just or unjust; neither is it whether this legal system in fact guarantees relatively peaceful conditions within the community constituted by the system. In presupposing the basic norm, no value transcending the positive law is affirmed.[170] Thus, the content of the law can be anything whatsoever.[171]

This contradicts the position represented by the argument from injustice, according to which norms that are unjust in the extreme cannot have the character of legal norms.[172] Not even this, however, is the downfall of the idea of a basic norm. One can add to the formulation of the basic norm a clause that takes into account the argument from injustice. A formu-

---

[168] See generally Alexy, *TLA*, at 221–86.
[169] See ibid., at 248–9.
[170] Kelsen, *PTL* § 34(c) (p. 201) (trans. altered)
[171] ibid. § 34(c) (p. 198) (trans. altered); see also Kelsen, *LT* § 28 (at p. 56).
[172] See above, this text, at 40.

lation that corresponds to the argument from principles as well as to the argument from injustice runs as follows:

If a constitution has in fact been issued and is socially efficacious, then, if and in so far as the norms of this constitution are not unjust in the extreme, it is legally prescribed that one behave in accordance with this constitution in such a way as corresponds to the claim to correctness.

This formulation refers only to the constitution. I shall examine norms issued in accordance with the constitution in the next chapter, on the definition of law.

(v) Tasks

That the basic norm has three altogether different tasks complicates the determination of its status.

(a) Transforming Categories

The first task of the basic norm is to make possible the transition from 'is' to 'ought'. Because 'is' and 'ought' are categories of altogether different kinds, this first task can be called '*transforming categories*'.[173] In that certain facts are interpreted as law-creating facts, the move into the realm of the law is accomplished.

(b) Setting Criteria

The move into the realm of the law could not be accomplished if the basic norm allowed the interpretation of any facts whatsoever—say, every expression of will that comes

---

[173] See Aulis Aarnio, Robert Alexy, and Aleksander Peczenik, 'The Foundation of Legal Reasoning', *Rechtstheorie*, 12 (1981), 133–58, 257–79, 423–48, at 142–6; Aleksander Peczenik, *Grundlagen der juristischen Argumentation* (Vienna and New York: Springer, 1983), at 23.

along—as law-creating facts. Thus, a second task is incumbent upon the basic norm. It must establish which facts are to be regarded as law-creating facts. In so doing, it sets the criteria for what law is. This second task can be described as '*setting criteria*'. Kelsen's criterion, as stated above, is that 'of a constitution that has in fact been issued and is by and large efficacious'.[174] Another variant of Kelsen's criterion is that of the 'historically first state constitution'.[175] Criteria like this include a reference, that is, they say that the criteria of the constitution are criteria for what valid law is. Thus, Kelsen can formulate his basic norm such that it is, first, very simple and, second, applicable to all developed legal systems. In Hart's theory, by contrast, the basic norm (rule of recognition) is identified with the rules of the constitution that say what law is. Hart's basic norm becomes thereby very complicated and is applicable only to the current legal system. The only thing general about it is that every developed legal system must have a norm like this. Both Kelsen's and Hart's criteria are positivistic. As stated above, the argument from injustice requires a restriction of positivistic criteria, and the argument from principles requires their supplementation.

(c) Creating Unity

The third task of the basic norm is to create unity.

All norms whose validity can be traced back to one and the same basic norm form a system of norms, a normative order. The basic norm is the common source of the validity of all norms belonging to one and the same system, their common basis of validity. A certain norm belongs to a certain system in that the ultimate basis of its validity is the basic norm of this system. This basic norm is what constitutes the unity of a multiplicity of norms by representing the basis of the validity of all norms belonging to this system.[176]

---

[174] Kelsen, *PTL* § 34(g) (at p. 212) (trans. altered).
[175] ibid. § 34(c) (at p. 200) (trans. altered).
[176] ibid. § 34(a) (at p. 195) (trans. altered).

It could be seen as a problem that the basic norms of developed legal systems are, in their content and their status, identical. Is it the same basic norm that creates the unity of each different legal system? How should that be possible? Or is it, after all, the constitution that leads to unity? These remain open questions here.

(vi) Status

The problem of the status of the basic norm concerns mainly its first task, transforming categories. As the norm that establishes the validity of all positive law, the basic norm cannot be in turn a norm of positive law.[177] But what is it then? One might think that then it could only be a non-positive norm and, as a non-positive norm, it would have to be a norm of either natural law or the law of reason.[178] Kelsen emphatically rejects that possibility. But what should the basic norm be if it is neither a norm of positive law nor a norm of suprapositive law, that is, a norm of natural law or the law of reason?

That this is not an easy question to answer is apparent not only in the boundless literature, but also in Kelsen's own doubts about the matter toward the end of his life.[179] His most significant answer is found in the second edition of the *Pure Theory of Law* (1960). There, four characteristics of the basic norm define its status.

(a) Necessary Presupposition

The first characteristic is that, if one wants to speak of legal validity or a legal 'ought', one must *necessarily presuppose* the

---

[177] See ibid. § 34(c) (at p. 199).

[178] See ibid., at § 34(i)(j) (pp. 217–21).

[179] See Hans Kelsen, 'Diskussionsbeitrag', *Österreichische Zeitschrift für öffentliches Recht*, N.F. (new series) 13 (1963), 119–20, repr. in *Das Naturrecht in der politischen Theorie*, ed. Franz-Martin Schmölz (Vienna: Springer, 1963) (same pagination).

basic norm.[180] In discussing the concept of the basic norm
above, it became clear that this thesis is correct in so far as one
must presuppose *some* basic norm if one wants to move from
ascertaining that something has been issued and is efficacious
to ascertaining that something is legally valid or legally obligatory. The discussion of the possibility and the content of
the basic norm has shown, however, that while this basic
norm must indeed include elements of the Kelsenian basic
norm, it has to be supplemented by non-positivistic elements.

Kelsen, because his basic norm is the necessary condition
for the possibility of the cognition of legal validity and the
legal 'ought', characterizes it, with a nod to Kantian terminology, as a 'logico-transcendental presupposition' of legal
cognition. This characterization is correct in so far as,
according to Kant, the transcendental is that which is necessary in order to make cognition of experience possible.[181]
Nevertheless, there is an important difference between the
transcendental in Kelsen and that in Kant, a difference manifest in the second characteristic of the basic norm.

(b) Possible Presupposition

The second characteristic is that one must indeed necessarily
presuppose the basic norm *if* one wants to interpret the law as
a normative system (an 'ought'-system), but this interpretation itself is only a *possible interpretation*.[182] As sociological

---

[180] See Kelsen, *PTL* § 34(d) (at p. 201); Kelsen, *LT*, at § 29 (p. 58).

[181] See Immanuel Kant, *Prolegomena to any Future Metaphysics* (1st
pub. 1783), trans. Peter G. Lucas (Manchester: Manchester University
Press, 1953), at 144 (trans. altered), *Ak* 4:373: '[T]he word transcendental ... does not mean something that goes beyond all experience, but something that, although it precedes (*a priori*) all experience, is not destined for
anything more than solely to make cognition of experience possible.'

[182] See Kelsen, *PTL* § 34(i) (at pp. 217–18); Kelsen, *Reine Rechtslehre*,
2nd edn. (Vienna: Franz Deuticke, 1960), § 34(g) (at p. 218 n.); ibid.,
Appendix, pt. 2: 'Die Naturrechtslehre', 402–44, at 443 (neither the long
note in § 34(g) of *Reine Rechtslehre* nor its Appendix is found in the English
translation).

and psychological legal theories demonstrate, it is possible even if for many purposes not very fruitful[183] to describe and to explain the law as a merely social and/or psychical concatenation of effects.[184] Kelsen himself emphasizes this when he comments that an alternative to the juridical interpretation of the law is a sociological interpretation, according to which the law is a system of 'power relations'.[185] One can therefore say that the basic norm is simply a possible or hypothetically necessary presupposition.

That is of consequence to its transcendental character.[186] In the area of experience, according to Kant, there are no alternatives, for example, to space and time as the forms of intuition. Cognition for Kant—that is, empirical cognition—is only possible, then, in space and time.[187] By contrast, cognition of legal phenomena is in principle also possible without the use of the category of 'ought'. Nevertheless, this does not fully dispose of the transcendental character of Kelsen's argument. While his argument cannot demonstrate, to be sure, the unconditional necessity of the basic norm and thereby the category of 'ought', it can show a conditional necessity. The juridical standpoint—or the standpoint of the participant in a legal system—is defined such that the law is interpreted by the participant as a valid system of norms or a normative system (an 'ought'-system). One can of course refuse, not only in action but also in thought, to participate in the (utterly real) game of the law. But if one gets into

---

[183] The interpretation of the law as a system of mere facts is not acceptable to a legal sociologist either; see Rottleuthner, *Rechtstheorie und Rechtssoziologie* (n. 144 above), at 31–61, 91–7.

[184] See Ralf Dreier, 'Bemerkungen zur Rechtserkenntnistheorie', in *MEA* 89–105, at 95.

[185] Kelsen, *PTL* § 34(i) (p. 218).

[186] See Stanley L. Paulson, 'The Neo-Kantian Dimension of Kelsen's Pure Theory of Law', *Oxford Journal of Legal Studies*, 12 (1992), 311–32, at 322–32.

[187] See Kant, *Critique of Pure Reason* (n. 143 above), at A24/B38 (p. 158): 'Space is a necessary representation, *a priori*, which is the ground of all outer intuitions'; and at A31/B46 (p. 162): 'Time is a necessary representation that grounds all intuitions.'

this game—and there are good reasons, at least in practice, to do so—then there is no alternative to the category of 'ought' and thereby no alternative to the basic norm. Thus, Kelsen's argument can be called a 'weak transcendental argument'. It shows that a basic norm (not necessarily Kelsen's) that introduces the category of 'ought' is the key to the realm of the law.

(c) Norm that is Thought

The third characteristic of the Kelsenian variant of the basic norm is that this norm is supposed to be only an imagined or a *thought norm*.[188] It must be this, for the basic norm as a willed norm would have to presuppose a further norm that would first of all transform the content of the willed into the content of an 'ought', since no 'ought' follows from the merely willed. And then the basic norm would not be the basic norm.

The first and second characteristics of the basic norm can be accepted. But here the problems begin, the first of which is the concept of a thought norm. Kelsen, in his later work,[189] rejected the thesis that the basic norm was simply the 'content of an act of thought'.[190] There is 'no "ought" without a will',[191] he wrote, so that 'along with a basic norm that is thought, an imaginary authority must also be thought... whose—fictitious—act of will has as its sense the basic

---

[188] See Kelsen, *PTL* § 34(d) (at pp. 203–4).

[189] Kelsen, 'Diskussionsbeitrag' (n. 179 above), 119: 'In my earlier writings... I represented my entire doctrine of the basic norm as a norm that is not the meaning of an act of will but, rather, that is presupposed in thought. Now I must unfortunately confess to you, gentlemen, that I can no longer maintain this doctrine, I have had to give it up.'

[190] Kelsen, *PTL* § 34(d) (p. 203) (trans. altered).

[191] Hans Kelsen, 'Die Funktion der Verfassung', in *Verhandlungen des zweiten österreichischen Juristentages Wien 1964*, vol. 2, pt. 7 (Vienna: Manz, n.d.), 65–76, 74. (This passage in Kelsen's article is not found in the English translation, n. 192 below, which is based on a shorter version of the same article.)

norm.'[192] Kelsen himself characterizes this notion as 'self-contradictory', for to say that the highest authority is empowered by a still higher—even if only fictitious—authority[193] is to say that the highest authority is not the highest authority. Moreover, a further basic norm would have to be invented to empower the fictitious authority to issue the basic norm, which would amount to not only denying the original basic norm its character as a basic norm, but also—since the further basic norm, too, could only be the content of an act of will—presupposing *ad infinitum* further fictitious authorities and the fictitious basic norms empowering them. This problem is not solved by Kelsen's thesis that a 'genuine fiction' is precisely what is at issue and that its being self-contradictory[194] is precisely what distinguishes such a fiction.

A solution can be found only if one gives up the notion that every 'ought' must be traceable to the willed. There are good reasons to do this. While an 'ought' is usually connected with the willed, there are exceptions. Thus, one can arrive at the view, based on considerations of fairness or justice, that one is morally obligated not to evade taxation, but one can at the same time continue to want to evade taxation and for that reason act contrary to one's insight into what is morally obligatory. Cognition of an 'ought' is necessarily attached neither to one's own act of will nor to another's act of will.[195] If this is correct, then the notion that the basic norm is simply a thought norm causes no difficulties.

A second problem is that of the normative or prescriptive character of a basic norm that is thought. Kelsen formulates the thought basic norm to say that one ought to do

---

[192] Hans Kelsen, 'The Function of the Constitution' (1st pub. 1964), trans. Iain Stewart, in *Essays on Kelsen*, ed. Richard Tur and William Twining (Oxford: Clarendon Press, 1986), 109–19, 117 (trans. altered).

[193] Hans Kelsen, *General Theory of Norms* (1st pub. 1979), trans. Michael Hartney (Oxford: Clarendon Press, 1991), ch. 59, § 1, D (p. 256).

[194] ibid.

[195] The semantic conception of the norm forms the basis of this thesis; see Alexy, *TCR*, at 21–5.

something: 'One ought to behave as the constitution prescribes.'[196] That is one side of the matter. The other side is
that, according to Kelsen, legal science prescribes nothing
when it bases its cognition of the law on this basic norm: 'It
does not prescribe that one ought to obey the commands of
the framers of the constitution.'[197] How is it possible that a
legal scientist, in formulating a sentence about what is legally
obligatory, necessarily presupposes that one ought to behave
as the constitution and thereby the law prescribes, while, on
the other hand, he does not prescribe with the formulation of
such a sentence that one ought to behave in accordance with
the constitution and thereby the law? The solution lies in the
concept of prescribing. Person *A* prescribes something to
person *B* when *A* demands of *B* that *B* do something.
According to Kelsen, the legal scientist qua legal scientist
demands of no one that he ought to behave in accordance
with the constitution and thereby the law. The legal scientist
can straightaway, qua legal scientist, give information about a
legal obligation and at the same time, qua human being,
demand that on moral grounds this legal obligation not be
met. The result is that the normativity of the law is hypothetical or relative in character. A legal scientist who gives information about a legal obligation does not say, 'You ought to
carry out act *a*.' Rather, the information he gives is, 'If you
take the standpoint of the law, then you are obligated to carry
out act *a*.' To be able to say this, and only to be able to say
this, the Kelsenian basic norm is needed: 'One ought to
behave as the constitution prescribes.' The legal scientist in
fact prescribes nothing thereby, for the decision to take the
standpoint of the law is left to whatever deliberations might
be entertained by the addressee of the legal scientist's statement. Above all, there is no prescription that the addressee
take the standpoint of the law. Rather, the attitude toward the
law is completely indifferent. There is a legal obligation only

---

[196] Kelsen, *PTL* § 34(c) (p. 201).
[197] ibid. § 34(d) (p. 204) (trans. altered).

for one who participates, for whatever reasons, in the game of the law. For one who does not participate, there exists only the risk of bearing the brunt of coercive acts. In this respect, the law imposes no obligations whatsoever. There can be no question that an interpretation along these lines is possible. The question is only whether it is adequate.

At many points in Kelsen's texts, there is only the most incomplete expression of the hypothetical or relative character of the normativity of the law. Accordingly, the conclusion of a basic norm syllogism is supposed to say, according to Kelsen, that one ought to behave in a certain way.[198] That gives the impression that the basic norm leads to a categorical obligation, independent of one's standpoint, which in turn can encourage the mistaken interpretation that Kelsen establishes with his basic norm a general obligation to comply with any and all legal norms. In the context of the basic norm, then, it is better to speak of a legal 'ought', not simply an 'ought'. Even then, the question remains open as to whether Kelsen's interpretation of this 'ought' is adequate.

(d) Incapability of Being Established

The fourth characteristic of the basic norm is supposed to be that it is *incapable of being established*: 'Into the basis of the validity of the basic norm there can be no further enquiry.'[199] This thesis is plausible on first glance. The basic norm as basic norm is the highest norm. A still higher norm would have to be presupposed if the basic norm should be established, but then the basic norm would no longer be the highest norm and therefore no longer the basic norm. On second glance, however, it is clear that this thesis is easily toppled. The basic norm at issue here is only the basic norm of the law. As the highest norm of the law, it cannot in fact be established by

[198] See ibid. § 34(d) (at p. 202).
[199] Kelsen, 'The Function of the Constitution' (n. 192 above), 112 (trans. altered); see Kelsen, *PTL* § 34(a) (at p. 195).

another norm of the law. That does not preclude, however, its being established by norms or normative points of view of a different kind, say, by norms of morality or through expediential deliberations. Kelsen could object that then these norms would be the basic norm of the law or these deliberations would have to be reformulated into a basic norm of the law. But that is not necessarily so. One can say that the move into the realm of the law is accomplished with the basic norm, and that there are moral or other extra-legal reasons for making this move.

To appreciate the error of Kelsen's thesis that there can be 'no further enquiry'[200] into the validity of his basic norm, one need only ask why every coercive order that is by and large efficacious should be interpreted as a legal system. Kelsen is right when he says that only if one presupposes his basic norm can one interpret as a legal system every coercive order that is by and large efficacious. But why should one interpret as a legal system every coercive order that is by and large efficacious? A reference to the basic norm is inadequate as an argument, for to presuppose the basic norm means precisely, after all, to interpret as a legal system every coercive order that is by and large efficacious. Since interpretation as a legal system and presupposition of the basic norm are two sides of the same coin, the one cannot be used as an argument for the other.

The question of why every coercive order that is by and large efficacious should be interpreted as a legal system, that is, why the Kelsenian basic norm should be presupposed, can be answered in very different ways. One answer has it that this is a matter of making a determination, a mere decision. That is not an argument, however. A second answer says that the presupposition of the basic norm is expedient. Individuals singly and collectively (say, as states) could orient themselves better and so take action more successfully if they adopted

---

[200] Kelsen, *PTL* § 34(a) (p. 195) (trans. altered).

this interpretation. That is an argument, but one might ask whether, of all the possibilities, the best presupposition for success is Kelsen's basic norm. A third answer is that the basic norm is required on moral grounds, say, that civil war is to be avoided. Here again the decisive question is whether the best moral argument truly leads to the Kelsenian variant of the basic norm. The argument from injustice, as discussed above within the framework of the critique of legal positivism, showed that there are good moral reasons not to ascribe legal character to everything that has been issued and is efficacious, and the argument from principles led to the conclusion that law is not only what has been issued and is efficacious. That will be taken up again in discussing Kant's basic norm. A fourth answer has it that Kelsen's basic norm expresses what always underlies the jurist's work in the law. This is an empirico-reconstructive argument that Kelsen himself approaches when he writes: '[The basic norm] simply raises to the level of consciousness what all jurists are doing (for the most part unwittingly)...'. But then he immediately takes leave of this view by adding: 'when they understand the law exclusively as positive law'.[201] The empirical question of whether or not jurists understand the law exclusively as positive law is not pursued by Kelsen. His thesis, therefore, to the effect that the basic norm simply raises to the level of consciousness what jurists are doing when they understand the law exclusively positivistically, is not an empirical claim. Rather than reconstructing the jurist's endeavour empirically, Kelsen's thesis explicates or defines the standpoint of the legal positivist. Not only is the question as to the correctness of this standpoint left open, the question as to the correctness of the description of the work actually done by jurists is not addressed either.

In summary, then, the following may be said about Kelsen's theory of the basic norm. Kelsen is right when he says

---

[201] ibid. § 34(d) (p. 205) (trans. altered); see also Kelsen, *LT*, at § 29 (p. 58).

that one must presuppose a basic norm if one wants to move from ascertaining that something has been issued and is efficacious to ascertaining that something is legally valid or legally obligatory. This basic norm, however, need not have the content of the Kelsenian basic norm. It may include moral elements that take into account the argument from injustice. Kelsen is also right when he says that while one must necessarily presuppose a basic norm if one wants to interpret the law as an 'ought'-system, one may forgo this interpretation. Thus, the character of the basic norm is only weakly transcendental. Finally, Kelsen is right when he says that the basic norm is simply a norm that is thought. He is not right, however, when he claims that the basic norm is incapable of being established. On the contrary, the basic norm needs to be established. And that leads to the problem of a normative basic norm.

B. The Normative Basic Norm (Kant)

Kant does not speak of a 'basic norm', nor is it at the centre of his—unlike Kelsen's—legal philosophy. Nevertheless, the idea of a basic norm is clearly formulated in Kant's *Metaphysics of Morals*: 'Thus, it is possible to conceive of an external legislation comprising positive laws alone, but then this legislation would have to be preceded by a natural law that established the legislator's authority (that is, the power to bind others simply by his arbitrary action).'[202] With that, the essential properties of a basic norm have been named. It is a norm that precedes positive laws, establishing the legislator's power to issue them and thereby establishing their validity. The decisive difference between Kelsen and Kant is that Kant's basic norm is not simply an epistemological presupposition, it is, rather, a 'natural law'. According to Kant, a

---

[202] Immanuel Kant, *Metaphysical Elements of Justice*, a trans. by John Ladd of pt. 1 of the *Metaphysics of Morals* (1st pub. 1797), 2nd edn. (Indianapolis: Hackett, 1999), 18 (trans. altered), *Ak* 6:224.

natural law is a law that, 'even in the absence of external legislation, can be recognized as binding, that is, can be so recognized *a priori*, by means of reason.'[203] Thus, Kant's basic norm is a norm of the law of reason, or—using an older terminology—a norm of natural law,[204] so that the validity of the positive law is established by the law of reason or natural law. This leads to the exact opposite of the morally indifferent character of the law in Kelsen's theory. It leads to a moral obligation to obey the law.

Kant's theory of the basic norm is embedded in the context of his legal philosophy, which is closely linked in turn to his moral philosophy.[205] I cannot even begin to present Kant's legal or moral philosophy here and shall look only at the reasons he adduces for his basic norm and at its content.

Kant's justification of his basic norm is part of his justification of the necessity of positive law, an argument in the tradition of social contract theories. These theories are marked by the distinction between a state of nature and what Kant calls a 'civil' state of affairs, that is, a legal or public state of affairs. Differences in the social contract theories are manifest, *inter alia*, in the interpretation of the state of nature. According to Kant, rights justified by reason already exist in the state of nature (*status naturalis*), but they are not secured in the state of nature. To secure these rights, there is supposed to be a dictate of reason that one leave the state of nature and move into a civil or legal state of affairs (*status civilis*):

So it is *a priori* in the rational idea of such a (nonlegal) state of affairs that, until a publicly lawful state of affairs is established, individual human beings, peoples, and states can never be secure against violence from one another, for each has his own right to do *what he deems just and good*, independently of the opinion of others. The first thing incumbent upon him, then, if he does not want to relinquish every conception of law, is to subscribe to the principle

---

[203] ibid. (trans. altered).

[204] See ibid., at 37, *Ak* 6:237.

[205] See Ralf Dreier, 'Zur Einheit der praktischen Philosophie Kants', in *RMI* 286–315.

that one must leave the state of nature, where everyone follows his own notions, and must unite with all others (with whom interaction is unavoidable) in subjecting oneself to a publicly lawful, external coercion. In other words, one must enter into a state of affairs where what is to be recognized as one's own is determined *by law* and is granted to one by an effective *power* that is not one's own, but an external power; that is, one should first of all enter into a civil society.[206]

One might think that this argument for the necessity of positive law leads to the conclusion that the natural rights that are supposed to be secured by positive law are somehow incorporated into the basic norm. But that is not the case. Kant's basic norm is exclusively oriented to legal certainty and civic peace. While it confers validity on the positive law, the content of that law is of no more consequence to Kant's basic norm than to Kelsen's. Kant makes this clear when he formulates his basic norm as a 'practical principle of reason' expressing the command that 'the presently existing legislative authority ought to be obeyed, whatever its origin'.[207] That leads to a strict priority of positive law over the law of reason, a priority justified by the law of reason. Kant's statements on the right of resistance and on the task of jurists are the clearest examples of this. A right of resistance is rejected: 'There is no legitimate resistance of the people, therefore, to the supreme legislative power of the state; for only through submission to the general legislative will is a legal state of affairs possible.'[208] On the task of jurists, Kant writes:

The jurist steeped in the text seeks the laws securing the *Mine* and *Thine* not in his own reason (when he acts, as he should, as a civil servant), but in the code of laws publicly promulgated and sanctioned by the highest authority. One cannot in fairness require him to prove the truth and the legitimacy of these laws or to defend them against the objections of reason. Decrees first and foremost make

---

[206] Kant, *Metaphysical Elements of Justice* (n. 202 above), 116 (trans. altered), *Ak* 6:312.
[207] ibid. 124 (trans. altered), *Ak* 6:319.
[208] ibid. 125 (trans. altered), *Ak* 6:320.

something legitimate, and now to enquire into whether the decrees themselves might also be legitimate is an absurdity that must be dismissed straightaway by the jurist. It would be absurd to refuse to obey an external and supreme will for allegedly failing to correspond to reason. The dignity of the government consists precisely in its insistence that, on questions of justice and injustice, subjects are not free to decide according to their own notions, but, rather, must decide according to precepts of the legislative power.[209]

Kant's strict priority of positive law over the law of reason, a priority justified by the law of reason, has been criticized again and again.[210] This critique can be supported by theses of Kant's that are irreconcilable—or at least hard to reconcile—with the notion that even a positive law that is unjust in the extreme has strict priority over the law of reason. For example, Kant reproaches a legal scholar whose orientation is purely empirical:

What is lawful (*quid sit iuris*), that is, what laws say or have said in a certain place at a certain time, can of course be stated by him [the empirically oriented jurist]. But whether the prescriptions of these laws are also just—indeed, what the universal criterion is that would make it possible to recognize what justice and injustice are (*iustum et iniustum*)—will remain obscure to him . . . Like the wooden head in Phaedrus' fable, a purely empirical theory of law is a head that may be beautiful, but alas, it has no brain.[211]

How can this be reconciled with Kant's view, cited above, that the question of the correctness or the justice of state laws 'is an absurdity that must be dismissed straightaway by the

---

[209] Immanuel Kant, *The Conflict of the Faculties* (1st pub. 1798), trans. Mary J. Gregor and Richard Anchor, in Kant, *Religion and Rational Theology*, ed. Allen W. Wood and George di Giovanni (Cambridge: Cambridge University Press, 1996), 233–327, 253 (trans. altered), *Ak* 7:24–5.

[210] See Ralf Dreier, 'Rechtsgehorsam und Widerstandsrecht', in *Festschrift für Rudolf Wassermann zum sechzigsten Geburtstag*, ed. Christian Broda, Erwin Deutsch, Hans-Ludwig Schreiber, and Hans-Jochen Vogel (Neuwied and Darmstadt: Luchterhand, 1985), 299–316, at 302–4, with further references.

[211] Kant, *Metaphysical Elements of Justice* (n. 202 above), 28–9 (trans. altered), *Ak* 6:229–30.

jurist'?[212] Doubts about the internal coherence of Kant's
theory are prompted, too, by his 'touchstone of the legitimacy
of each and every public law',[213] which says: 'What a people
cannot resolve for itself cannot be resolved for the people by
the legislator either.'[214] Is it really so, that this criterion can
never restrict the obligation to obey the law, not even in cases
of tyrannical caprice? Is it really definitive that legal certainty
and civic peace require compliance with each and every state
law, even one of extreme injustice, utterly contemptuous of
what Kant calls the 'sole original right belonging to every
human being by virtue of his humanity', namely, freedom?[215]
The discussion of the argument from injustice has shown that
this kind of unlimited priority of positive law must be rejected.
Laws that are unjust in the extreme must be denied legal
character.[216]

What does all this mean for the evaluation of Kant's basic
norm? There are two possibilities. The first is preferred by
those who say that Kant's basic norm corresponds best to the
basic principles of Kant's philosophy. The basic norm would
be subject, then, to criticism based on points of view outside
the Kantian system. The second possibility is preferred by
those who say that Kant's basic norm is neither a necessary
nor the best conclusion to draw from the basic principles of
his philosophy. This thesis can be connected to the claim that
the obligation to obey that is required by Kant's basic norm
fits better into the Kantian system when the obligation is
restricted by means of a criterion like that of Radbruch's
formula than when it is unrestricted as in Kant's own strict
version of his basic norm. A theoretico-interpretative insight

---

[212] See Dreier, *Rechtsbegriff und Rechtsidee* (n. 139 above), at 10.

[213] Immanuel Kant, *On the Common Saying: That May be Correct in
Theory, but it is of No Use in Practice* (1st pub. 1793), in Kant, *Practical
Philosophy*, trans. and ed. Mary J. Gregor (Cambridge: Cambridge Univer-
sity Press, 1996), 273–309, 297 (trans. altered), *Ak* 8:297.

[214] ibid. 302 (emphasis omitted) (trans. altered), *Ak* 8:304.

[215] Kant, *Metaphysical Elements of Justice* (n. 202 above), 38 (trans.
altered), *Ak* 6:237.

[216] See above, this text, at 40–62.

at this point might be that not even a great philosopher always draws the correct conclusions from his own basic principles. Which of these two possibilities is preferable in evaluating Kant's basic norm cannot be considered here in the requisite detail. So there is only this conjecture, namely, that Kant, in strictly formulating his basic norm, has not drawn a conclusion that is definitively prescribed in his system, but, rather, has succumbed to contemporaneous notions of the authoritarian state.[217] If this conjecture is correct, then Kant's basic norm is to be modified in terms of the argument from injustice. If this conjecture is incorrect, then Kant's basic norm, justified by the law of reason, is more positivistic in its effects than Kelsen's basic norm. Kelsen's basic norm says only that one can, if one wishes, interpret every issued and efficacious norm as a legally valid norm, without thereby giving rise to any moral obligations whatsoever. By contrast, Kant's basic norm would say—unless it were restricted—that one must interpret every issued and efficacious norm as a legally valid norm regardless of whether or not one wishes to do so and, moreover, that one is morally obligated to obey every such norm. A morally justified radical positivism like this is far less acceptable than Kelsen's sceptical, epistemological variant.

C. THE EMPIRICAL BASIC NORM (HART)

The essential points of a critique of Hart's basic norm have already been covered in discussing Kelsen's basic norm. Nevertheless, the eminent role played by Hart's basic norm in the literature and its status, alongside a basic norm of the Kantian type, as the most important alternative to Kelsen's basic norm demand a systematically comparable statement.

Hart speaks not of a 'basic norm' but of a 'rule of recognition'. He grants that his theory of the rule of recognition is

---

[217] See Dreier, 'Bemerkungen zur Rechtserkenntnistheorie' (n. 184 above), at 93.

similar in some respects to Kelsen's conception of a basic norm.[218] He justifies his differing terminology with, above all, the different status of his basic norm.[219]

The consonance of the two theories is unmistakable. Hart's rule of recognition comprises the criteria for identifying rules as valid law[220] (he speaks of 'rules' instead of 'norms'). It is the ultimate rule of the legal system.[221] As such, it comprises the criteria for, and thereby the basis of, the validity of all other rules of the legal system, that is, the validity of all rules excepting itself.[222] As with Kelsen's basic norm, one reaches Hart's rule of recognition by enquiring, within the hierarchical structure of the legal system, into the basis of legal validity at every level. Hart demonstrates this with an example in which the last answer and thereby the formulation of the apposite rule of recognition is, '[W]hat the Queen in Parliament enacts is law.'[223]

Every bit as obvious, however, are the differences between the two theories. The most important difference is that the question as to the existence of a rule of recognition as well as the question as to its content are empirical questions.[224] '[T]he rule of recognition exists only as a complex, but normally concordant, practice of the courts, officials, and private persons in identifying the law by reference to certain criteria. Its existence is a matter of fact.'[225] This is supposed to be the reason one can speak only of the existence of the rule of recognition and not of its validity. While it is indeed the criterion for the validity of all other rules, it supposedly cannot, as the highest criterion for validity, be in turn valid itself.[226] Its existence is said to be *shown* in the way participants in a legal system identify rules as valid law.[227]

[218] Hart, *CL* 245, 2nd edn. 292.   [219] ibid.
[220] Hart, *CL* 97, 2nd edn. 100.   [221] Hart, *CL* 102, 2nd edn. 105.
[222] Hart, *CL* 104, 2nd edn. 107.   [223] ibid.
[224] Hart, *CL* 245, 2nd edn. 292.   [225] Hart, *CL* 107, 2nd edn. 110.
[226] Hart, *CL* 105–6, 2nd edn. 108–9.   [227] Hart, *CL* 98, 2nd edn. 101.

On first glance, this appears to be an irresistibly simple solution to the problem of the basic norm. But it is too simple, as became clear in the discussion of Kelsen's basic norm. Hart infers the existence of the rule of recognition from its acceptance, manifest in legal practice, and then uses its existence as the basis for the validity of all other legal rules. The crucial problem lies in the concept of acceptance. To accept a rule that finds its expression in a common practice is to move from the fact that the practice exists to the conclusion that it is commanded that one behave in accordance with this practice. The advantage of the Kelsenian theory of the basic norm is that this transition from 'is' to 'ought' is not hidden behind concepts like the acceptance and existence of a practice, but is held up to the light and turned into a theme. An empirical theory of the basic norm must fail in the end, for it cannot adequately come to terms with the essential problem of every basic norm theory—the transition from 'is' to 'ought'.[228]

---

[228] See Ralf Dreier, 'Sein und Sollen', in *RMI* 217–40, at 223.

IV

Definition

The results of the arguments developed here can be brought together in a definition:

> The law is a system of norms that (1) lays claim to correctness, (2) consists of the totality of norms that belong to a constitution by and large socially efficacious and that are not themselves unjust in the extreme, as well as the totality of norms that are issued in accordance with this constitution, norms that manifest a minimum social efficacy or prospect of social efficacy and that are not themselves unjust in the extreme, and, finally, (3) comprises the principles and other normative arguments on which the process or procedure of law application is and/or must be based in order to satisfy the claim to correctness.

This is a definition of the law from the participant's perspective[229] and thereby a juridical definition of the law. The defined concept of law includes the concept of validity.[230] The three parts of the definition correspond to the arguments from correctness, from injustice, and from principles, respectively.

The *first* part of the definition contains as a defining element the claim to correctness.[231] A system of norms that neither explicitly nor implicitly lays claim to correctness is not a legal system.[232] In this respect, the claim to correctness has a classifying significance.[233] This has few practical consequences, for actually existing legal systems regularly lay claim to correctness, however feebly justified the claim may be. Practically speaking, what is more important is the qualifying significance[234] of the claim to correctness. Accordingly, simply failing to satisfy the claim to correctness does not exact legal character or legal validity from legal systems or individual legal norms, but, rather, renders them legally defective.[235]

---

[229] See above, this text, at 25.
[231] See above, this text, at 35–9.
[233] See above, this text, at 26.
[235] See above, this text, at 35–6.

[230] See above, this text, at 23–4.
[232] See above, this text, at 34.
[234] See above, this text, at 26.

That is an expression of the fact that there is necessarily an ideal dimension to the law.

In the *second* part of the definition, the relation of the three classic defining elements to one another is specified—authoritative issuance, social efficacy, and correctness of content. The relation is specified on two levels, that of the constitution and that of norms issued in accordance with the constitution. Expressed thereby is the fact that the definition has a limited range. It applies only to developed legal systems manifesting a hierarchical structure. A simplified variant of the definition would have to be worked out for legal systems that are not developed, but this is not pursued here.

A condition for the validity of a constitution is that the constitution be by and large socially efficacious. This formula refers to the social validity of the legal system as a whole, for a constitution is by and large socially efficacious only if the legal system as a whole that is established in accordance with the constitution is by and large socially efficacious.[236] The concept of a social efficacy that exists 'by and large' also includes characteristics named in many definitions of the law—coercion and dominance over competing systems of norms. The characteristic of coercion is included in that the social efficacy of a norm consists in either compliance with the norm or, in the event of non-compliance, the imposition of a sanction, which includes the exercise of physical coercion, a task reserved to the state in developed legal systems.[237] The characteristic of dominance over competing systems of norms is included in that a system of norms that does not prevail in a conflict with other systems of norms is not by and large socially efficacious.[238]

What has been said thus far on the validity of the constitution—that is, on the first level of the second part of the definition—is also true of positivistic legal concepts. This part

---

[236] See above, this text, at 89–90.
[237] See above, this text, at 85–6.
[238] See above, this text, at 90.

of the definition is non-positivistic in that the criterion for the by and large socially efficacious constitution is restricted by the negative definitional characteristic, injustice in the extreme. The basis for this restriction is the argument from injustice.[239] It should be emphasized that the characteristic, injustice in the extreme, differs from that of social efficacy in that it applies not to the constitution as a whole, but, rather, only to individual norms of the constitution.[240] This is an expression of the fact that the legal validity of a legal system as a whole depends more on social validity than on moral validity.[241]

At the second level of the second part of the definition, the focus is on individual norms issued in accordance with the constitution. This second level is necessary, for, unlike legal systems, individual norms need not be by and large socially efficacious as a condition for their legal validity. That criterion is replaced in a hierarchically constructed legal system by the criterion of authoritative issuance in accordance with a constitution that is by and large socially efficacious.[242] There are two restrictions on this criterion. Authoritatively issued individual norms forfeit legal validity if they do not manifest a minimum social efficacy or prospect of social efficacy or if they are unjust in the extreme.[243] The latter is again an expression of the non-positivistic character of the concept of law presented here.

While the positivistic concept of law is restricted in the second part of the definition by the definitional characteristic, injustice in the extreme, the *third* part of the definition expands the sphere of what belongs to the law by including in the concept of law the process or procedure of law application.[244] Everything on which an official applying the law in the open area of the law bases and/or must base a decision in order to satisfy the claim to correctness belongs to the law.[245]

---

[239] See above, this text, at 40–62. [240] See above, this text, at 62–8.
[241] See above, this text, at 92–3. [242] See above, this text, at 91.
[243] See above, this text, at 40–62, 91. [244] See above, this text, at 24–5.
[245] See above, this text, at 68–81.

So it is that principles, even when they cannot be identified as legal principles according to the validity criteria of the constitution, as well as other normative arguments justifying the decision become components of the law. The clause 'bases and/or must base' gives expression to the interplay of the real and the ideal dimensions of applying the law. The law includes those arguments on which officials applying the law in fact base their decisions, even if these decisions do not measure up to the claim to correctness, and it also includes those arguments on which the decisions would have to be based in order to satisfy the claim to correctness. A critique of the practice of making legal decisions becomes thereby possible from the standpoint of the law.

Index of Names

Index of Subjects

Lightning Source UK Ltd.
Milton Keynes UK
UKOW031545190613

212487UK00008B/138/P